W9-ATS-282

# THE BIRTH OF THE AMERICAN TRADITION IN ART

I

MRS. ELIZABETH CLARKE FREAKE AND HER BABY MARY

# THE BIRTH OF THE AMERICAN TRADITION IN ART

---

OSKAR HAGEN

F.R.S.A., HONORARY FELLOW UNIVERSITY OF GÖTTINGEN
PROFESSOR OF THE HISTORY OF ART, UNIVERSITY OF WISCONSIN

ILLUSTRATED

---

KENNIKAT PRESS, INC./PORT WASHINGTON, N. Y.

BIRTH OF THE AMERICAN TRADITION IN ART


Reissued in 1964 by Kennikat Press by arrangement
with Charles Scribner's Sons.

Manufactured in the United States of America

Library of Congress Catalog Card No: 64-24458

*In memory of Thyra*

*to*

MAX AND RHODA OTTO

# Preface

THE PRESENT VOLUME covers the history of painting in America from about 1670 to the Revolution. Some day I hope to bring this history down to present times.

The facts which I have brought together to demonstrate the birth and the early development of the American tradition in art are not in the conventional sense biographical or encyclopedic. The questions to which I have tried to find answers are raised by the problems of artistic form; they are answered not by the life stories of a host of painters, but by the paintings that were produced by a few leaders who furthered the American tradition constructively. I have not discussed the less original painters or those who were but the tail-enders of obsolescent traditions.

I wish I could have written this history of the evolving American tradition without any reference to biographical matters. But for such a departure the time has not yet come. The biographies of some of the leading painters of colonial America still need a good deal of clarification and rectification. Where it was unavoidable, I have branched out into such discussions; at times even at great length. Gaps had to be filled in the story of John Smibert. The chronology of his early career in Scotland and England is here represented for the first time and so is the important episode of his life at the court of Cosimo III, the Grand Duke of Tuscany. Likewise, the life story of Robert Feke has been tentatively reinterpreted in such a manner that its documentary evidence makes sense. Moreover, without biographical investigations I would have been unable to achieve one essential objective of this book, namely, the depiction of the European background of colonial American art which has been sadly neglected in all the earlier literature. Occasionally my excursions had to be extended into quite distant history—in the case of the English antecedents to the period of Henry VII. I trust that such surveys will not be mistaken for compilations from other authors. My interpretation of the development of English art in the Tudor and Stuart periods and its relation to the contemporary continental trends is, I believe, new in both the approach and the findings. However, my picture of the artistic London in the days of West and Copley would not be what it is without the vast amount of new data furnished in William Thomas Whitley's several volumes on the subject, especially that invaluable source of information entitled *Artists and Their Friends in England, 1700-1799*.

These biographical excursions, incidentally, have helped to evaluate the relative significance of the leading painters in the upbuilding of the American tradition. Where the development of that tradition is under question, it is imperative to ascertain which artists were of American fiber and furthered the tradition, and which were of European fiber and retarded or destroyed the tradition's growth. My investigations bear out the fact that the contributions of Robert Feke were more constructive than the contributions of John Smibert; and that John Singleton Copley, who carried the colonial ideal to its classic consummation, was the most constructive force in the whole history of colonial art, in contrast to Benjamin West, who advocated quite alien ideals and was the most deflective force.

I am deeply grateful to friends, colleagues and graduate students who have furthered my manuscript by their critical advice. Above all, I wish to express my gratitude to the dear friends to whom the book is dedicated for their faith, encouragement and constructive criticism; to Doctor Curtis P. Nettels, historian of *The Roots of American Civilization*, Mr. Lee Simonson, artist and historian of the American stage, Mr. Homer Saint Gaudens, and Doctor W. D. Howe for their forthright support of my application for aid to The American Council of Learned Societies; to Miss S. Elizabeth De Voy, art editor of Charles Scribner's Sons, for her wholehearted co-operation on the illustrations; to the owners of the paintings for their kind permission to reproduce them here (in each instance credit is given in the List of Illustrations); and to Holger E. Hagen for helping me read the proofs. A grant of The American Council of Learned Societies has made possible the publication of this book.

OSKAR HAGEN

The University of Wisconsin.

# Contents

## CHAPTER ONE

## THE ARCHAIC PHASE OF COLONIAL ART



## CHAPTER TWO

## JOHN SMIBERT



## CHAPTER THREE

## ROBERT FEKE

CONTENTS

## CHAPTER FOUR

## JOHN SINGLETON COPLEY IN NEW ENGLAND



## CHAPTER FIVE

## BENJAMIN WEST



## CHAPTER SIX

## COPLEY IN EUROPE

# Illustrations

# ILLUSTRATIONS

# ILLUSTRATIONS

# ILLUSTRATIONS

# ILLUSTRATIONS

# THE BIRTH OF THE AMERICAN TRADITION IN ART

CHAPTER ONE

# THE ARCHAIC PHASE OF COLONIAL ART

## I. *The Colonial Background*

"THE EARTH is the Lord's and the fullness thereof; the world, and they that dwell therein." As an illumination of these lines from the Psalms, Albrecht Dürer, in 1515, drew on one of the vellum pages of the prayerbook of Emperor Maximilian I the earliest known picture of an American Indian. Seventy-one years later, John White, one of the hundred and seven men who set up Raleigh's first colony, drew the aborigines of Virginia and Florida from life; his colored drawings, frequently exploited for book-plates in stories of travel, are now in the British Museum. Remarkable though they are, Dürer's invention and White's ethnographic studies have nothing to do with the beginnings of American art. There was no American art until art was produced in North America for local consumption. Its birth dates from the founding of Jamestown and Plymouth.

Inasmuch as arts and crafts came from the Old World and since they disregarded whatever autochthonous arts or crafts were produced by the natives, the question arises, whether one may speak of the *birth* of American art. Yes, I think one may. Hellenic art, too, was born from what its fathers, invading Greek territory in centuries of migrations, brought with them from northern Europe.

As in every other primitive civilization, artistic enterprise in America originated with the crafts. Glass blowers came to make beads for the Indians. Potters, weavers, painter-stainers and other artisans furnished daily necessities. Silversmiths followed in due time. In 1650 three of them were already working in Massachusetts: John Mansfield and Robert Sanderson, who were experienced crafters before they came here, and John Hull, who received his training in the colony. In 1645 Jeremiah Dummer, the first native silversmith, was born in Newbury.

Nearly as old as these crafts was signboard painting, the venerable ancestor of our pictorial advertising. It had a big vogue in England from the sixteenth century, or even earlier. Projecting on wrought-iron arms from inns, shops, or private houses, pictorial signs were then what street numbers are today. The fad lasted until it became a menace to passers-by and was prohibited. Since the settlers continued their English habits in their new environment, it is a safe assumption that the streets of New England resembled gaudy picture galleries quite as much as did the villages of old England. To produce the signs, there must have been sign painters in the colonies at an early date. No unusual talent was needed; any one could paint a sign. But in case a painter did have unusual talent, that did not exclude him from the job. It may be taken for granted that painters, no matter how skilled, did not refuse to paint a signboard if they were fortunate enough to receive an order for one. Thomas Child, known as a well-trained "face painter" from his likeness of *Sir William Phips* (Boston, Mass., William T. Gardiner, Esquire), used to stain window frames and shutters, paint gates, fences and entire houses, and "prime and finish" cannon carriages.[1] This was toward the end of the century, but it will hardly have been different at the beginning. In the old country artists would perhaps have turned down such lowly jobs. In the colonies, where an artist was regarded as a parasite anyway, they had to accept anything that earned them an honest penny.

New Englanders did not have much use for "art" if it was "more for ornament than necessity." "The plowman that raiseth grain is more serviceable to mankind than the painter who draws only to please the eye," wrote an unknown New Englander in 1719.

A good deal of controversial discussion has been printed in regard

[1]*Seventeenth Century Painting in New England* (Worcester, Mass., 1935), pp. 114 ff.

to the Puritan's contempt of art.[2] With more than four hundred likenesses extant of people born in New England and New Netherland before 1700, but with every other class of painting missing for the same period, there can be no doubt that portrait painting was reckoned among the arts not any more than photographs of friends and relatives are nowadays. This inference is further borne out by the fact that family likenesses were not mentioned in wills; only one portrait is mentioned in the inventories of the seventeenth-century estates of New England.[3] Obviously portrait painting was considered just one of several possible ways of commemorating persons of interest, then as later. "For a few people who desired to make visible their rise in life, portraiture was, in the eighteenth century, as serviceable as householding or silversmithing; the founding fathers of the nation were preceded by the founding fathers of families who required effigies equally with furniture as a means of consolidating and maintaining their social position."[4] Such utilitarian ideas were a stumbling block to later painters who had a higher conception of art. Copley complained that "was it not for preserving the resemblance of particular persons, painting would not be known in the place; the people generally regard it no more than any other useful trade."[5] Perhaps the early settlers were not entirely wrong in classifying portraiture with the useful trades. For the most part, early colonial likenesses were "art" in the sense that early colonial literature, especially that of the divines, was "literature." In both cases the meaning counted more than the form in which it was represented. That is why mediocre talents and igno-

[2] *Art in America,* edited by Holger Cahill and Alfred Barr, Jr. (New York, 1935), maintains in one place that "the Puritans had no love for art and no time for its practice" (p. 6) and in another that "the Puritans had no such aversion to art as is commonly ascribed to them" (p. 9).

[3] *Seventeenth Century Painting in New England, op. cit.,* p. 12.

[4] Virgil Barker, *A Critical Introduction to American Painting,* New York (Whitney Museum of American Art), 1931, p. 14.

[5] *The Letters and Papers of John Singleton Copley and Henry Pelham, 1739–1776,* Mass. Historical Society Proceedings, Vol. 71 (1914), p. 65.

ramuses could venture forth as "artists." Only in portraiture, as William Hogarth said, "a man of very moderate talents may have a great success, as the artifice and address of a mercer are infinitely more useful than the abilities of a painter."

The limitations of art to "face painting" were fostered by the economic conditions in the colonies. In the wilderness of North America one did not set out on the uncertain path of limning unless he was reasonably sure of making a part, if not all, of his living thereby. In that regard face painting has always been preferable to other artistic performances; "it is the chief branch of the art by which a lover of money can get a fortune" (Hogarth).

The getting a fortune was a good way off in early New England and a painter's life was no bed of roses. Specific case histories are not available until nearly the middle of the eighteenth century. But it stands to reason that the practice of art was handicapped in the rude setting of the seventeenth century more seriously than it was a century later. No limner could make any sort of living if he depended exclusively on a clientele of townspeople; he had to go on the road. And so, from the very beginning, the itinerant limner became the rule. If he was a sensitive person, the hardships to which he was exposed in the almost unbroken wilderness, and the rough company he encountered in the taverns, must have been disheartening.

Added to this was the difficulty of obtaining brushes, palettes, canvases, and stretchers. In England these utensils were for sale at any paintshop. In the new country one had to make them with his own hands. Artists were lucky if they could purchase a supply of house paint. More often they were forced to resort to blueing, berry juices, or Indian war paints. As late as the mid-eighteenth century, young Benjamin West clipped the cat's tail and fixed the hairs in a goose quill for a paint brush. The want of the most elementary tools and media compelled colonial limners to equip themselves betimes with the frontiersman's resourcefulness and—the quack's contempt for professional training.

## THE COLONIAL BACKGROUND

Painted likenesses made a very early appearance in America. Many were no doubt imported. Family likenesses belong to the class of heirlooms that one does not readily leave behind on transferring to his new home. As Richard Mather, in 1635, brought along the high-chair in which he sat as a child, so Nicholas Roberts, in 1675, brought no less than eight ancestral portraits to his new abode. In fact, any likeness now in America that antedates the year 1665 is suspected of being foreign work. In some instances the sitters never visited the colonies; in others, they left them too early to be portrayed there; again in others, European authorship must be inferred from the superior technique of the painting under question.

It is inconceivable that the artist who painted *Sir Richard Saltonstall* (Boston, Mrs. Richard Saltonstall), or the Rembrandt pupil who portrayed *Peter Stuyvesant* (New York, Historical Society), would have gone unnoticed and unrecorded had they really rubbed shoulders with the colonial limners of whom we shall hear presently. A number of the portraits that were shown in the memorable exposition of "New England Painters of the Seventeenth Century" at Worcester, Mass., in 1934, have been recognized as foreign work, for instance, the *Simon Bradstreet* (Boston, Athenæum) as the work of a student of Rembrandt. I would add that the *Dr. John Clark,* of 1664 (Boston, Medical Library, Fig. 9), is closely related in point of style to the *Doctor of Medicine,* of 1663, in the Picture Gallery of Dulwich College, a painting by Pieter Nason of Amsterdam (Fig. 10).

The demand for painted likenesses no doubt fluctuated, depending on the class of people who immigrated. We must remember that the average social level was not the same at all times. The gentleman adventurers who came to Virginia with Captain Smith appreciated the amenities of life that lay outside the reach of the later tobacco growers to whom John Pory referred, in 1619: "In these five moneths of my continuance here there have come at one time or another eleven sails of ships into this river; but fraighted more with ignorance, than with any other marchansize." Again, the great stream of Puritans that sought refuge from the heavy hand of Archbishop Laud carried well-educated men, if not "the best," as John Richard Green believed—John Cotton who had been lecturer, dean and catechist at Trinity College in Cambridge; Harry Vane, son of a secretary of state under Charles I; John Winthrop, Roger Williams, *et al.* Among the 20,000 Englishmen who crossed the sea before 1640, many may have been rabble; but some, surely, had the breeding and taste that qualify a prospective art consumer.

## II. *British Antecedents*

Certain peculiar traits and idiosyncrasies that eventually marked the American tradition in art were already prominent at the time when art first began to sprout in New England and New Netherland. As long as these traits are ignored, the roots of the American tradition remain hidden. If its growth is to be comprehended biologically—which is the historian's supreme duty—those roots must be bared and examined. Speaking less metaphorically, a survey of the antecedents of American art, however summary, is imperative. This will clear up a number of mysterious matters that have, so far, been taken for granted though obviously they cry out for comment.

For example, if signboards are left out for the time being, why was likeness painting the only accepted vehicle of expression in the colonies? Religious themes were, of course, taboo; and for historical paintings there was as yet no history. But why no other class of picture—landscape or genre painting? This must seem strange, considering the novelty of the New England scenery, the picturesqueness of Indian life, the flora and the fauna of the New World. Technical inability on the part of the producers and moral bias on the part of the consumers may answer part of our question, but they do not answer all of it.

The unique limitation of early colonial painting to portraiture seems less strange if we consider the historical ties that linked New England to the mother country. In the era of Charles II, when art was first produced this side of the Atlantic, England, alone of all

European nations, continued to confine her artistic production almost exclusively to likeness painting. She had done so since the Reformation. The continent could boast an art rich in regard to subject matter, covering the religious stories of the Scriptures, the Golden Legend, and the devotional lore of Our Lady; an equally wide range of pagan mythology, landscape, marine, still-life, and genre subjects. But in England subjects other than likenesses were admitted only in exceptional cases. Pictures the least bit suggestive of popery were demolished with the monasteries under Henry VIII. Hans Holbein's brave efforts to introduce allegorical murals did not have a following under the zealous supervision of Queen Elizabeth. Puritanical bias purged England of every other kind of secular art. The nation that eventually counted Hogarth, Gainsborough and Wilson among her greatest artists did not, before the eighteenth century, have any use for either genre pictures or landscapes.

In the evolution of British likeness painting two successive traditions must be distinguished: Tudor and Stuart. Each lasted for approximately a century. The former culminated under Elizabeth, the latter under Charles II. The Elizabethan style matured after a struggle of many years between the medieval, insular taste and the continental vogue of the renaissance. Crudely speaking, the issue was the æsthetic aspects of likeness painting. Which was more desirable—illusionistic plasticity, as the continent wanted it, or decorative flat design, as England wanted it?

When Hans Holbein first came to England, in 1528, his bulky manner of representation was poles apart from the surface decoration then prevalent in English portraits, such as *Lady Margaret Beaufort,* mother of Henry VII (*circa* 1470, London, National Portrait Gallery, Fig. 14). What likenesses he had painted previously, for example, *Lais* (1526, Basel, Public Art Gallery, Fig. 13), were charged with all the voluminosity that body, robe and setting would yield. Instead of spreading his lines flatly like a cobweb over his panel, Holbein exploited every device of line, shading and color for the attainment of a strong three-dimensional effect. Note the incessant contrasts of light and dark, the foreshortened hand, the rearward slant of chest and shoulders, the windowsill in front and the curtain in back of *Lais*. No compromise seemed possible between this continental "sculptural" approach and the English gentle surface music that shunned modelling shadows and did not even allow a pair of hands folded in prayer to display plastically their foreshortening.

Yet, in the sixteenth century a compromise had to be reached if foreign artists wished to enlist English patrons. A comparison of Holbein's latest likenesses with others that he painted during the early years of his sojourn in England leaves no doubt as to the painter's submission to the English practice of flat lighting and linear ornamentation—witness, his *Anne of Cleves* (1539, Louvre, Fig. 15).

The ultimate emancipation of the Tudor tradition from the continental is registered even more graphically in the work of Nicholas Hilliard, sergeant painter to Queen Elizabeth. The queen's scant respect for continental realism is well documented by her comments to Hilliard on the continental chiaroscuro painters and by her demand that he paint her likeness "in the open alley of a goodly garden where no tree was near nor any shadow at all."[6] The miniature of *Queen Elizabeth* (Fig. 16), flat and lacy as a butterfly's wings, shows to what extent Hilliard, in stressing planarity and linear ornamentation, surpassed Holbein—whose manner, incidentally, he admired and professed to imitate.

The queen's criticism of artists abroad and the manner of art she sponsored at her court put it beyond doubt that she was determined to restore the medieval style. The very fact that the Late Tudor style was "legislated" explains why all that had been naïve and unstudied in the authentic medieval manner of presentation now assumed symptoms of artful contrivance. The Elizabethan

[6]*Treatise on the Art of Limning* (1624), Hilliard's book, discussed by Sir Richard Holmes in *The Burlington Magazine,* VIII (October–March), 1905–1906.

style was the British branch of *manierismo* and is, therefore, the most revealing cue to the puritanical mentality of the age. As it invariably happens when an escape from the present into the past is attempted, the present was not hidden under the medieval mask it wore. On the contrary, the present became more conspicuous as it shone through, and face and mask combined disclosed the lack of ingenuity, the warpedness, the repression, of the Elizabethan age. The decorative charm which lingered in the portrait of *Margaret Beaufort* changed to decorous rigor in the portraits of her great-granddaughter. In contrast to the genuinely medieval style of the fifteenth century, the medievalized mannerism of the "Cobham portrait" of *Queen Elizabeth* (London, National Portrait Gallery, Fig. 24) discloses a blend of incompatibilities quite as cramped as the Puritanism of which, unwittingly, it was an expression: on the one hand, a filigree of planar ornamentation and unshadowed coloration—in other words, a sublimation of reality; on the other hand, a minute record of every tangible detail which, when it comes to the queen's uncomely physiognomy, borders on ruthlessness. The only thing comparable to this blend of sublimation and reality will be found in the New England limning, three score and ten years after the death of the Virgin Queen.

The medieval manner was continued for provincial consumption until well after the Restoration of the Stuarts, but at the court of Charles I it was superseded by a cavalier's style given to splendor and ocular deception. Exactly as on the continent, perspective was stressed, figures were embedded in soft atmospheric luminosity, and color was made a vehicle of plastic expression. A slight change in that direction was already apparent during the latter part of the reign of James I, but the true originator of the Stuart tradition was Anthony van Dyck, who came to the court of England exactly one hundred years after Holbein's appointment to Henry VIII, and brought with him the painterly means by which to express that "pomp and glamour of outward show" which his master, Peter Paul Rubens, was so surprised to find when he visited England in

1629.[7] Not until van Dyck's permanent transfer to London, in 1632, did English portrait painters learn all the tricks of flattery and prevarication for which the Tudor regime had nothing but contempt.

Small wonder that the frosty rigor of the old tradition melted when Sir Anthony told the king and his cavaliers to deport themselves as befits perfect gentlemen, namely, with easy grace. The pose assumed by *King Charles* in his famous full-length picture in the Louvre (Fig. 17) was indeed without precedent in English art: the body in profile, one arm foreshortened and resting on the hip, the head thrust around to face the spectator. To unstiffen the sitter, to make his movement seem liquid, van Dyck introduced an entire stock of new gestures: that thrust of the head forward from foreshortened shoulders—often accompanied by a fetching glance at the audience, particularly if the model was of the other sex; differentiated action of the arms to break the monotonous spell of Elizabethan symmetry; a hand advancing as in spirited conversation to dramatize the character.

Van Dyck's several pupils picked up these histrionics eagerly and preserved them—Sir Peter Lely still under Charles II. Lely made van Dyck's manner more palatable for court consumption. He knew his master's tricks in and out, but, in addition, he had an eye for certain Anglicisms that eluded his Flemish master—extreme polish, voguish grace, and studied superficiality. His development, never determined by personality, reminds one of a clever cook who elaborates standard recipes to satisfy the fickle taste of his patrons. The simile describes Lely especially well at the time when the puritanical restrictions of the Commonwealth came into force and, again, when they were invalidated to make room for the gay times of Charles II. To what degree Sir Peter displaced van Dyck's authenticity by a mere exhibition of sensuous appeal may be gleaned from his *Lady Byron* (Hampton Court, Fig. 18), one of the "Windsor Beauties" of the 'sixties; not from the complicated pose

[7] *Die Briefe des Peter Paul Rubens* (ed. Otto Zoff), Vienna, 1918, p. 361.

and rapturous expression alone, but from the fastidious color orchestration—persimmon red with orange, blue with gold and *puce,* brown and black.

Apart from bringing new attitudes and gestures, van Dyck changed the whole Elizabethan manner of staging a portrait. Pompous settings came into sway—columns set against a distant landscape, impressive marble steps for the models to ascend, bulging draperies, and liquid patterns of composition in which the rich flow of light blended with the model's facial expression, pose, and gesticulation. To realize the fluidity of such a group as Peter Lely's *Family of Sir Edward Hales* (Fig. 22), we should remember how, only half a century earlier, Marc Ghaeraedts lined up *Lady Sidney and Her Six Children* (1596, Penshurst; Fig. 21), as though they were so many of the hoary stones of Stonehenge.

It is quite conceivable that the Puritans, who left England when Lely was the rage, did not relish his sensuous manner and why, therefore, no reverberation of his art is found in early New England. It is less conceivable why they did not accept the more sober and unflorid manner of the Commonwealth painters. For during the Civil War, under the Protectorate and until the Restoration, the exuberance and flamboyance of Sir Anthony van Dyck's English school was set aside. It was not extirpated; Lely's temporary catering to the taste of the Roundheads did not last a day longer than the return of the Stuarts. But the Stuart tradition was concealed for the time being. Other artists, trained under the influence of Philippe de Champaigne and the French Jansenists—the Puritans of the Roman Catholic Church—stepped forward and practised portrait painting in a style that was more in keeping with the new ethical and moral codes.[8]

[8]Jansenism had much in common with Puritanism; it rose from disgust with the laxity of the times and was opposed to the Jesuits and the court. Philippe de Champaigne, the painter of the movement, cultivated a style severe, sober and factual. His sitters were made to pose in clear and simple views. Symmetry was a predominant rule in his compositions. Verticals and horizontals controlled his design. Ornamental trappings were rigorously curbed. With documented

An exemplar of that manner was Robert Walker, a Puritan by conviction and a close friend of Oliver Cromwell whose life dates he shared (1599–1658). Walker's three-quarter length, *Oliver Cromwell and His Squire* (London, National Portrait Gallery, Fig. 23), represents the victor of Marston Moor, the commander of the Ironsides to whom enemies were but "stubbles to their swords," in a manner different from anything that issued from van Dyck's school. For one, Walker did not stake the effect on the voguish accouterment of his model; van Dyck's *Charles* (Fig. 17) compares with Walker's *Cromwell* as a fashion plate compares with analysis of character. Though Cromwell's armor was of importance in the construction and expression of the portrait, Walker did not characterize his man by his clothes so much as by his head—one of the most comprehensive character heads in the history of British painting; a *likeness* truthful to the limit. There is honest reference to "the countenance swoln and reddish" mentioned by Sir Philip Warwick, and on it the two opposing traits of Cromwell's character are unmistakably engraved: his melancholy and physical frailty, as well as the third, the energy with which he held the other two in check. But what dominates is the eyes—irritable, feverish, almost despondent eyes. It is apparent, too, that Walker hated "ornamentation" almost as much as van Dyck's followers relished it. The bulky figure barely fits into the frame. There is nothing of the conspicuous waste of space that was fashionable with the Stuart painters and one must

biographical data as scant as they are, my contention is hypothetical and will probably never be verified beyond doubt, namely, that the Commonwealth manner, which did not evolve organically from the Stuart manner but took its place for a little more than a decade, was determined by the influence of de Champaigne. Surely, Isaac Fuller, whose rollicking temperament was anything but puritan, must have been under the influence of something like *Le prévot et les échevins de la ville de Paris* (Louvre), before he could find the unornamented geometric composition and the serious mood of his *Family of Sir Thomas Browne* (Devonshire House). The similarity resides in the whole approach so radically different from the flamboyant, "decorative" portrait groups fashionable in Stuart court circles immediately before the Revolution; *e.g.*, *Lely's Family of Sir Edward Hales* (Fig. 22).

remember their boisterously draped and sheeny robes to appreciate fully the monotonous effect of Cromwell's black suit of armor, its unyielding and unrelieved outline, its surfaces broken up only here and there by a few metallic flashes of reflected light. It is a portrait worthy of a man of deeds, not of words.

Which of the British schools, then, influenced the archaic phase of New England portraiture? That it was not the van Dyckean trend has already been pointed out; Restoration art smacked too much of a sybaritic court to be to the liking of Puritans and Nonconformists. The Commonwealth painters should have been the logical source of influence, but, strange to say, no trace of Robert Walker or John Michael Wright can be detected. The nearest thing of which the New England limners of the last quarter of the seventeenth century remind one is the Elizabethan tradition. And what could be more natural than that immigrant painters from England should imitate Tudor art and immigrant patrons ask for such imitation? In England, moreover, both Stuart and Commonwealth pictures were less accessible to painters of low social rank than Elizabethan paintings. Portraits of ladies and cavaliers passed directly from the studio to the mansion and were not seen by the public, unless they were publicized by engravers, which was quite rare in seventeenth-century England. Art exhibitions were unknown. Provincial work, however, was accessible in lowly country houses of the Restoration period and there the Elizabethan vogue was not out of date as at court. In the little English towns from which the settlers came, portraits had been preserved for generations; moreover, new ones, then as nowadays, were most likely painted in an old-fashioned manner. Rustic painters, even if they had any knowledge of the "latest" movement in art, hardly took stock in its vagaries.[9]

[9]Unfortunately provincial painting in Great Britain has never been made a special objective of research. The exclusive interest of critics and public in a few "great names" explains why photographs of provincial paintings are al-

But before building any theory on what may in the end turn out to be but a superficial resemblance, let us approach the incunabula of New England painting and examine them somewhat more closely.

### III. *Limners in Seventeenth-Century New England*

No indigenous portrait in New England, so far as we know, was painted before about 1670. In the subsequent twenty-odd years at least seven limners were active in Boston or within a radius of about thirty miles of it—a fairly large number, considering that Boston was a provincial town of a population of slightly over 4000.[10]

Of Joseph Allen only name and occupation are known.[11] Three others may be identified in regard to both their names and their work: Thomas Child, Thomas Smith, and—if critics will give up unnecessary scruples—Jeremiah Dummer. The remaining three are known only by their work. Following a time-honored custom of my trade, I suggest christening each of these anonymous limners after his most characteristic painting. In the following I shall distinguish: (1) The John Davenport Limner; (2) The John Freake Limner; and (3) The Limner of the Mason Children.

First, in point of time, comes the Davenport Limner, who may have been John Foster of Dorchester (1648–81); the question hinges on the likeness of *Richard Mather,* teacher of the church of Dorchester, who died in 1669. The painting, owned by the American Antiquarian Society, is in an exceedingly poor state of preser-

most unobtainable, why illustrated catalogues, even where such curios are exhibited, fail to reproduce the interesting small fry, and why the abundance of provincial work in countless private English homes is still uncharted. Specialists of British painting and its history disregard them, not however without relieving their conscience with a nice little excuse like this: "This history is not the place for treating the unnumbered obscure portrait painters."

[10]According to the estimate of Carl Bridenbaugh, *Cities in the Wilderness,* New York, 1938, p. 6.

[11]Alan Burroughs, *Limners and Likenesses,* Harvard University Press, 1936, p. 24 f., tentatively attributes five portraits to Joseph Allen, the dates of which extend over almost half a century.

vation, but from it was made, by Mather's friend, John Foster, an ungainly wood-engraving, the first of its kind in America. The author of the engraving may well have also executed the painting. At any rate, whoever did the likeness of Richard Mather also did the likenesses of three divines: the New Haven pastor, *John Davenport* (1670, Yale University Museum, Fig. 12); the Salisbury pastor, *John Wheelwright* (1677, Boston State House); and the portrait of an unknown clergyman for some time erroneously called *John Cotton* (1670 or 1679, Historical Society of Connecticut, Fig. 11).[12] The three last-named likenesses are humble, sincere attempts; dearthful of color, poor of design; comparable, at best, to fifth-rate English provincial productions. Still, these likenesses and those of the "Limner of the Mason Children"[13] are not readily forgotten for their naïve characterization.

The "Freake Limner" was quite another fellow. A primitive who may rank with the most sensitive designers and colorists of fourteenth-century France or fifteenth-century England. His activity in New England cannot be traced through more than about five years. Five paintings can be attributed to him with certainty: *John Freake,* and *Mrs. Elizabeth Clarke Freake and Baby, Mary* (on loan at The Worcester Art Museum, *circa* 1674, Fig. 1); and three *Gibbs Children,* Margaret (Fig. 28) and Henry (Mrs. Al. Q. Smith, Charleston, W. Va.), and Robert (T. J. Damon, Esq., Concord, Mass.). Less certain, but in my opinion likely, is the attribution of the portraits of *Edward* and *Rebecca Rawson* (Boston, New England Genealogical Society, Fig. 26) to the same painter. The large *Elizabeth Paddy Wensley* (Plymouth, Pilgrim Hall, Fig. 25), though equal in quality, is not by the Freake Limner.

The group of *Mrs. Freake and Her Baby* (Fig. 1) shows that the

[12]See the lengthy discussion in *Seventeenth Century Painting in New England, op. cit.,* pp. 55 ff.

[13]Portraits of *Mrs. John Quincy as a Girl* (circa 1677, Quincy, Mass., Adams Memorial Society) and *Children of Arthur Mason* (Boston, estate of Paul Mascarene Hamlen, Esquire; and Quincy, Adams Memorial Society).

artist was a true colorist. The picture should delight any one, provided he stops thinking of "unity," "balance" and such-like "rules," of which this colonial primitive was as unmindful as a songbird is of the rules of *bel canto*. The Freake Limner combined the naïveté of archaic Greek and medieval artists with a somnambulant instinct for brittle delicacy of expression. As often in productions by non-professional painters, his color chord is not readily memorized. One has to look twice before one associates its unconventional multiplicity of *terre verte,* bright and dark red, greenish yellow, gray, black, and pallid flesh tints. His accents often seem to be but accidents, for instance, that lovely surface of red-brick patterned with fine silver and gold ornaments in the left-hand foreground. Such "unruly" things betray the "archaic" American artist, the "independent" who would rather turn over a new leaf and begin from scratch than continue the closing chapter of European painting.

The uniformity of style in all the pictures that have been mentioned is so marked that it outweighs certain differences in the application of pigments to the canvas, or the greater or less use of modelling shadows; differences which occasioned Alan Burroughs to separate an "English" from a "Dutch" group of seventeenth-century limners in New England. If the bulk of these paintings is viewed in the perspective of European art of the late seventeenth century, their stylistic homogeneity should be clear beyond doubt. The design of the portrait of *Mrs. Freake and Her Baby,* which on account of its flat lighting is supposed to exemplify the "English" group, is just as rectilinear, angular, and rigid as the portrait of *Mrs. Martha Patteshall and Her Child* (*circa* 1674, Boston, Miss Isabella Curtis) which, on account of its chiaroscuro, is supposed to exemplify the "Dutch" group. Both are equally far removed from any European manner of the sixteen-hundred-and-seventies, especially from the flamboyant and liquid Stuart tradition of England. In point of conception, composition, design, lighting, and coloration, the two pictures are equally different from van Dyck's version of the mother-and-child theme[14] and equally similar to its Tudoresque version.[15]

This curious resemblance once led me to believe that the archaic limners of New England stemmed from the Tudor tradition. A superficial comparison of, say, the portrait of *Elizabeth Paddy Wensley* (Fig. 25) with, say, the "Cobham portrait" of *Queen Elizabeth* (Fig. 24) seems to reveal enough stylistic analogies to put the matter beyond doubt. Upon closer inspection, however, it becomes apparent that my theory must be qualified in certain ways.

To begin with, the flatness of the Pilgrim Hall portrait had other causes than the planarity of the Elizabethan style where similar effects were attained by deliberate omission of modelling shadows. In the colonial painting the effect came from the artist's ineptitude to view and represent an ensemble. If, as here happens to be the case, every individual finger, arm, chin or eye-socket is separately as well as timidly designed and modelled, instead of contrasting one mass broadly with the other, then these forms inevitably lose their coherence and the figure as a whole fails to detach itself from the ground. Let us distinguish this plane-*boundness* of the colonial primitives from the plane-*consciousness* of the Elizabethan artists. In the latter instance avoidance of plasticity was an æsthetic ideal, whereas the primitive limner did not know any better. His honest though unsuccessful endeavors to build up every separate form in the round make it evident that plasticity was his aim, but what he got, due to his unskilled technique, was flatness.

Another distinguishing mark is the coloration of the Pilgrim Hall likeness. Whoever may have been the painter of the "Cobham portrait" of *Queen Elizabeth* was a "knowing" artist and a true exponent of the refined Late Tudor style. His sparing display of color was sophisticated, in fact, almost affected; note the offish harmony of closely related chromatic values, that variety of shades

[14]Compare Van Dyck's *Wife and Daughter of Colyns de Nole* (Munich, *Alte Pinakothek,* Fig. 20).

[15]Compare Paul van Somer's *Lady Apsley and Son* (Cirencester House, Fig. 19).

of brown offset with black and white. Now, the color scheme of the *Elizabeth Wensley* is also based on brown (a reddish ocher paint used for the modelling has something to do with that), but this general tone was obviously an accident rather than an intended expression of reticence. Everywhere there are signs of a primitive pleasure in patches of motley color. The canvas is gay as a bunch of autumn leaves. Red, green and white are interspersed. Tulips, carnations, and white roses on a red tablecloth make a brilliant spot in the lower left; green stripes enliven the dress; the underskirt is lined with pink.

Such profound stylistic differences have made it clear to me that my earlier theory of a wholesale derivation of colonial limning from Elizabethan art is untenable.

Some critics have not associated the limners of Massachusetts with the English school at all. They have taken the Freake Limner for a Dutchman. Francis Henry Taylor[16] suggested he might have been French and influenced by "Jansenist" portraits. Mr. Taylor pointed out that Oxford, Mass., where the Freake family owned land, was one of the first Huguenot refuges in the colonies. Huguenots were known as good craftsmen, but had nothing in common with Jansenism. Hating Roman Catholicism as they did, it is quite improbable that any artist of Huguenot faith should have joined the school of Philippe de Champaigne. Moreover, the small body of Huguenots who settled in Oxford, but soon removed to Milford, did not come until 1687, that is, at least thirteen years after the Freake portraits were completed. Of course, the influence could have travelled to New England in many other ways. As Virgil Barker pointed out,[17] it could have come via Quebec where seventeenth-century portraits of a decidedly French taste have been traced. It could also have been spread through prints. In contrast to England, where engraving was in its infancy in the second half of the seventeenth century, France at that time was in a golden

[16] *A Guide to the Collections of the Worcester Art Museum,* 1933, p. 94.
[17] "Puritan Portraiture," in *The American Magazine of Art* (October), 1934.

age of graphic art. Her portrait engravings, which were, without exception, reproductions of paintings, were the finest in all Europe and many of her leading masters were pupils of Philippe de Champaigne, *e.g.,* Jean Morin, Robert Nanteuil, and his countless assistants.

Nevertheless, with nothing better than such guesswork to buttress the hypothesis, the derivation of the Freake Limner's manner from Jansenist portraiture seems less likely than from the Elizabethan English school. There are too many improbabilities involved. A Roman Catholic, painting New England worthies around 1670–75, is an absurdity. But supposing the Freake Limner had been a Protestant self-taught in the French tradition and without knowledge of its religious significance or symbolism—then, are the stylistic similarities between his and "the Jansenist portraits of the Loire Valley," to which Mr. Taylor refers, such that they warrant associating the French with the American school? A certain tender charm in the half-smiling face of *Mrs. Freake* (Fig. 1) and a sense of précieuse decoration in the outlines and the ornamental handling of frills, such as the ribbon around the neck of *Rebecca Rawson* (Fig. 26) or the little bows on the sleeve of *Mrs. Freake,* may faintly suggest the gothic stone carvers of Reims, or Clouet and Watteau. But there the similarities end. The style of Philippe de Champaigne, from whom alone one may learn what Jansenist painting was, contained *plasticity* as the one essential element. And precisely that element is wanting in the flat work of the Bostonian. This alone precludes his association with the French seventeenth-century school quite as much as with the Stuart painters of England. Sincere, plainspoken characterization, scrupulous attention to external details, rigid composition, angular design, avoidance of excessive ornamentation—all these traits might pass as possible evidence of a Jansenist influence on the early colonial limners as they did for the English Commonwealth painters. But without *plasticity,* as an expression of bodily presence, Jansenist portraits would not be what they are. The absence of three-dimensionality and chiaroscuro goes to show that the Freake Limner did not study, and probably never saw, French works of art either in the old country or in the New France. What little I have seen of Canadian portraits of the seventeenth century is quite unlike the New English. In contrast with their New England contemporaries, the Quebec painters imitated to the best of their ability the voluminosity of the French school.

The preceding check-up on current theories as to the probable dependence of the colonial limners on European schools has proved that none of the analogies yields conclusive evidence that New England painting originated either from the Elizabethan or the Jansenist traditions. As a matter of fact, the stylistic similarities may be purely accidental. Personally, I am convinced that early colonial painting was less dependent on European art than is commonly believed.

At this point I should like to lay bare what seems to me the gravest mistake on the part of the historians of colonial art. They have slighted the significant fact that the limners were not professional artists, but were what we call *Sunday painters*. Critics have often commented on the poor craftsmanship of some colonial painters and rightly so; there can be no doubt that the John Davenport Limner would have been doomed to oblivion elsewhere. On the other hand, the John Freake Limner would have held his own even if his competitors, instead of being untrained provincials, had been experienced Londoners. But all that is beside the point. What distinguishes a professional artist from a Sunday painter is not so much a difference in the quality of their achievements as a difference in the degree of their dependence on tradition. Professional painters respect the tenets and theories of the schools in which they were reared. Sunday painters are outsiders. As more recent experiences have shown, they were all independents—the customs employee Henri Rousseau in nineteenth-century Paris, the freight-car painter John Kane in twentieth-century Pennsylvania, and many other lay painters all over the world; so independent were they that their respective manners cannot be traced to the influence of any professional school or tradition.

Obviously, it would be absurd to approach colonial primitives as though they had been Giottos or Raphaels, and to employ, without qualification, methods of research which have been tested only on artists who, by training and social position, were members of tradition and school. Giotto and Raphael were artists, and artists alone; with careers planned accordingly. Their training would have made them unfit for the tinker's or tailor's profession. They were apprenticed in their most impressionable age to past masters of art in whose shops for many years they imbibed tradition and learned every trick of the trade. For another few years they went as journeymen abroad, serving other masters until, ultimately, after they were admitted as free masters to their guild, they were allowed to train pupils of their own and impart tradition to them. That sort of historical continuity—an indispensable premise where the dependence of one school upon another is under question—is completely missing in the early phase of colonial art. In contrast with the great ones just mentioned, our Boston primitives were not ripples on a continuous stream of evolution any more than afterwards were Joseph Pickett of New Haven, Pa., Adolf Dietrich of Germany, Camille Bombois, Louis Vivin, and Séraphine of France, or unnumbered similar "lay painters" of Russia and the Americas, none of whom was influenced or determined by academic theory and its painted examples.

If the works of these lay painters are jointly viewed, they reveal a uniform primitiveness which seems not to have altered at all through the centuries, because these painters-by-avocation were not connected at any time with period fashions. Besides being untrained, they did not pay the slightest attention to the "problems" with which the schools were grappling.

One explanation for their lack of interest in the ruling trend was that art was not their real trade. Bombois has been a street-paver, Vivin a postal clerk, Séraphine a washwoman, Dietrich a lumberjack. Nor was art the trade of the New England limners who could not live on what little money they got in return for an occasional portrait or two. Poor economic conditions in the colonies forced them to make a livelihood out of some other more remunerative business. When the limner was more fundamentally an artist by inclination and talent, he could manage to eke out his income by practising a side-branch of "the painting business," as in his time John Smibert did who ran an art store. In many if not in most cases, it is likely that the artistic urge was not there to begin with. As the demand for likenesses grew, the grocer, the tinker, the scythe-maker, added limning as a fairly profitable extension to his ordinary business. Countless advertisements in colonial news-sheets give evidence of this peculiarly American blend of commerce and art. In 1711, Abraham Delancey of New York thus notified customers: "Old Madeiras and other wines, groceries, and most kind of painting done as usual at reasonable rates." In 1744, one John Pringle of Charleston, S. C., advertised "a choice collection of books, pictures, and pickles."

Incidentally, it was such colonial practices which made American artists for a long time to come dependent on the demand of the lay public. In order to sell their pictures at a profit they played up to their patron's taste, whether they agreed with it or not. Unwittingly, the art consumer who buys pictures as he buys persimmons and pickles has determined the course of the development of art in America in a much larger measure than he has in Europe, where pictures and pickles were never mentioned in the same breath, not even if the pictures were by lay painters.

In contrast to the nineteenth-century lay painters, who lived unnoticed amidst the multitude of professional artists, limners were the only "artists" in the early colonies. Cultural conditions there produced and encouraged, almost automatically, the practise of art by non-professionals. A very significant fact, it seems to me.

My investigations have demonstrated the futility of any endeavor to trace archaic colonial art to specific sources of influence, whether it be the Elizabethan art of England or the Jansenist art of France. This clears the way for further endeavors. Instead of hunting for European influences, the beginnings of our national art must be approached as something independent and underived. Analysis of the archaic style, not its derivation, is the historian's first assignment.

## IV. *Sunday Painters Defined*

"Sunday painters" are not the same as "amateur painters." Amateurs, or *dilettanti* as they were called in the eighteenth century, practise a hobby for their own delectation. Sunday painters work for gain. Like quacks, they practise a trade with the pretensions of a professional, but without his qualifications; also, as I have just pointed out, without his interest in what is seasonable. It is in this respect that the difference is particularly evident. Dilettantes always trail some fashionable manner of representation—generally yesterday's. Sunday painters, however, do not heed the changing manners of art. Lay art does not grow in the shadow of academies; it can exist in the wilderness. When business in the grocery or in the workshop was running low, the boss turned limner in the colonies and painted likenesses as fishermen whittle spoons and figureheads when a lull in the wind keeps them idle. That is why lay painting resembles folk art.

And just as folk art practically never changed its manner, so the structure of lay painting is today what it was three hundred years ago and probably long before that. Period styles do not apply to lay paintings. Only by external criteria can one tell to what period one of them belongs; for instance, by the fashion of dress or the style of the buildings represented in the picture.

What, then, is the peculiar structure of lay painting?[18]

First. Lay painting, like the art of children, knows but the uni-

[18]Studies on the subject are: Franz Roh: *Zum Begriff der Laienkunst,* in *Cicerone,* XVIII (1925), pp. 472 ff.—Nikola Michailow: *Zur Begriffsbestimmung der Laienmalerei,* in *Zeitschrift für Kunstgeschichte,* IV (1935), pp. 283 ff.

versal and typical. It eliminates all the nuances, transitions and irregularities which, in the opinion of professional painters, constitute individuality in life. Only on that hypothesis was it possible that certain limners, before offering their services as portrait painters to persons they had never before seen, prepared in advance dummy likenesses that contained everything except the faces—the dress, flowers, jewelry, the setting and, quite often, even the hands. The "family resemblance" of persons who posed for one limner at different places and times is further evidence that typicalness was all a colonial Sunday painter cared about.

The concept "typical" also covers a variety of characteristics pertaining directly to the edited form of colonial as well as more recent lay painting. With this I mean the rigid view of the model from in front, stereotyped attitudes, gestures and accessories. As to sameness of pictorial arrangement, compare *Rebecca Rawson,* of 1675 (Fig. 26), *Mrs. Elizabeth Drake Fuller* (Fig. 29) and the *North-German Lady* (Fig. 27) of the early nineteenth century. The concept further covers certain technical procedures in editing the pictorial form, such as inflexible design and primary colors unbroken and unmodelled. Very similar generalizations were achieved by dint of callow perceptual forms in the Freake Limner's *Gibbs Children* (Fig. 28) of the end of the seventeenth century, the *Girl with Roses* (Whitney Museum of American Art, Fig. 30) by an unknown American of about 1830, and Henri Rousseau's *Girl in the Wood* (Fig. 32), of the end of the nineteenth century.

Second. Lay painters isolate their objects. They ignore the visual integration of a multitude of different things and forms. Above all, they disregard the atmospheric envelope that joins colors into a harmony and unites figures with their setting. Therefore their inclination toward the typical never induced them to represent things in a sweeping manner. Nothing was more alien to them than broad sketchiness or the "tone painting" of professional schools. In fact, they never could represent mass. If perchance an archaic colonial landscape picture should turn up, I am sure it would show the same isolated houses with separate window frames and separate panes of glass, the same trees with separate limbs and leaves, the same human or animal figures spelled out detail for detail, which are found, silhouetted and dispersed across the width of the picture, in Vivin's *Conseil d'Etat,* of 1925 (Fig. 33) and in Joseph Pickett's *Coryell's Ferry, 1776* (Whitney Museum of American Art, Fig. 35).

Third. Lay paintings do not give the impression of being records of something really seen. They do not depend on actual perception so much as on mental ideation. I am not saying that the primitives did not observe. They were concerned with the phenomenal world; but even if they "looked" at their objects all they wanted, they still were unable to "see" them correctly. The *Girl with Roses* (Fig. 30), Henri Rousseau's *Past and Present* (Fig. 31), Dietrich's *Garden* (Fig. 36), Pickett's *Coryell's Ferry, 1776,* and John Kane's *Across the Strip* (Washington, D. C., Philipps Memorial Gallery, Fig. 34)—all these pictures of diverse countries and times are ideographs projected from a thousand and one images stored in the painter's mind.

This brings us to points four and five.

A lay painter's ideation does not honor correct drawing; correct is that which need not fear comparison with nature as seen. None of the figures drawn by the primitives under discussion is accurate as regards proportions or organic structure. The ideational method prohibits correctness. Only one who thinks instead of sees will represent children as diminutive adults or express the vastness of a landscape by peopling it with pygmies.

But notwithstanding their inaccurate drawing, the outlook of lay painters is fundamentally factual. It is quite misleading to point out "the bold departure from reality" in the paintings of Henri Rousseau. The error comes from the inability of professional artists to understand the full measure of naïveté back of the paintings of the "little customs clerk." Neither Rousseau nor any other lay painter aimed at "abstract art." Least of all our colonial limners whose likenesses were first and last complete inventories of the sitter's property, his furniture, dress and jewels. If limners employed undifferentiated local colors and sharp contours in editing their pictures, the reason was that they knew of no better method to state beyond doubt that the person represented wore this, that, or the other typical color of dress; that the objects around were of this, that, or the other typical form. If the colors had been correctly graded or broken in conformity with atmospheric lighting, this would not have become sufficiently clear. If their outlines had been submerged in a shadow, the persons would have lost in identity.

At first, such a combination of materialism and ideography may seem inconsistent. In reality it is quite consistent. For the ideational method, applied uniformly to every object, does to the perceptual form what a common denominator does to a mathematical equation. This ideational method was never mixed with the experienced painter's observational method. Therefore colonial likenesses, despite the manifold objects they represent, never fall apart as do any number of neo-primitive portraits of today. Grant Wood's *Woman with Plants* (Fig. 38) was done in emulation of the primitives by a twentieth-century sophisticate. His conscious effort to resume primitivism came into conflict with his advanced experience. Therefore the *Woman with Plants* lacks the unity and correlation which came without struggle to the unknown nineteenth-century itinerant who painted *The Lady Holding a Book* (Whitney Museum of American Art, Fig. 37). In Mr. Wood's portrait the two methods are employed side by side and, of course, refuse to blend. The lady's head and hands are meticulously observed from life, but the dress with the rick-rack apron, and the landscape, are ideated or, if you prefer the word, conventionalized.

To make this analysis complete, I should add that, apart from the lay painter's relation to nature, we must also consider his relation to his media.

Panel and canvas proper cast something like a magic spell on the imagination of untrained painters. The flatness of the painting surface had a great deal to do with their drawing a frontal view of the sitter, the rectangular shape of the stretcher is largely responsible for their blocking out the entire form in a similar rectangular oblong, and the emptiness of the canvas tempts them to fill every square inch of it and, if the model does not afford enough form, to resort to planimetric ornamentation.

## V. *Followers of the Stuart Tradition in New England*

Captain Thomas Smith and Jeremiah Dummer trailed the Stuart and Restoration painters of England. Does this indicate a general departure at the end of the seventeenth century from the independence of the limners of the 'seventies or was it only a case of two derivative amateurs? Unfortunately there is no way of telling. The fact that their names and a few items of their personal history are known makes them only slightly more tangible than the unnamed limners.

Did Thomas Smith express the views of a somewhat later period than the Boston limners? Only one of his paintings is dated, namely, the three-quarter length of *Major Thomas Savage,* of 1679 (Boston, Mass., Henry L. Shattuck, Esquire, Fig. 39). A likeness of *Doctor Ames,* mentioned, on June 2, 1680, in the treasurer's account book at Harvard University, has perished. The rest of his work has been tentatively ascribed to the 'eighties and 'nineties.

He came as a mariner from Bermuda sometime in the middle of the century. Eight lines in rime in a corner of his *Selfportrait* (American Antiquarian Society, Fig. 41) tell that in advanced years his heart turned from the world's "Jarres, Joies, Toies, Wyles and Warrs." But we are left guessing what particular experiences molded his fine old face. The range of his development was astonishingly wide. But was it a development or just an erratic shifting from one manner to another?

In 1679 he was imitating the Commonwealth painters of London. The compositional formula of the *Major Savage* (Fig. 39) was almost identical with that of Robert Walker's *Oliver Cromwell* (Fig. 23). But Smith's imitation clearly betrays the amateur. He did not achieve the voluminosity of the professional painter. Beside the well-rounded *Cromwell, Major Savage* looks as flat as a plank. And while Smith did shade the face and the hands more than the archaic limners, his shading was timid. The whole manner of his drawing here and in the *Captain George Curwen* (Essex Institute, Salem, Mass., Fig. 40) still definitely reminds one of the planarity as well as the angularity of the early 'seventies.

As a seafaring man, Captain Smith probably saw a good deal of the world and, being an amateur of the arts as well, seems to have imitated whatever happened to appeal to him of European portraits. Hence the desultoriness of his manner. When the *Self-portrait* and the likeness of *Maria Catherine Smith,* the painter's daughter, were first shown side by side in the Worcester Museum, it seemed difficult to believe that two pictures so unlike in conception and execution should have been painted by one individual. The *Selfportrait* betrays familiarity with Flemish methods; it is elaborately "designed" and very precisely modelled by means of differentiated explanatory shadows. The portrait of *Maria Catherine* (Fig. 42) is broadly "painted" and, except for the lavish drapery, is almost unmodelled. Instead, it is built up on color–indeed, on a very unusual color chord. It reminds me of Spanish painting. Perhaps a Saint Catherine by some Murillo imitator, accidentally preserved in a Spanish American mission, inspired father Smith to paint his daughter in this utterly foreign color combination–an almost black-brown for eyes and hair, and a turbulent copper-red, becoming pure orange in spots, for the dress. Color chords are sometimes quite as revealing as dialects; the Venetian color dialect differed from the Florentine about as much as the spoken Venetian differed from the Tuscan. The violent color chord of this likeness sounds vaguely "Andalusian" to me. At any rate, there is nothing like it in the coloration of Lely or Kneller, to whose schools the picture has been most generally related.

Jeremiah Dummer of Newbury, Mass. (1645–1718), holds a fourfold record in the early history of American art. He was the first silversmith who was born in the colonies; the first colonial silversmith who combined his profession with engraving; the first native painter whose name is known; his *Selfportrait* of 1691 is the first dated and signed painting by a native of Massachusetts. Some critics who insist that Jeremiah Dummer was nothing else but a silversmith have voiced doubts as to the authenticity of this and three other portraits of his. Alan Burroughs[19] has put forth the arguments that speak for and against Dummer's paintings. In my opinion the fact that Dummer was also a painter needs no other evidence than the inscription on the back of the *Selfportrait* owned by Messrs. Nathaniel and Devens Hamlen (Fig. 43). The very lettering, as several authors have stated, corresponds to other authentic autograms of Jeremiah Dummer that have been preserved, for instance in the Historical Society of Boston. The same handwriting appears on three other portraits, of 1691 and 1708 respectively; to wit, the portrait of *Mrs. Anna Atwater Dummer* (Messrs. Nathaniel and Devens Hamlen, Fig. 45) and the portraits of Mr. and Mrs. John Coney (privately owned in Gloucester, Mass.). The evidence of Dummer's authorship furnished by the inscriptions is stronger than what has been considered counter-evidence, namely, the lack of uniformity in the technique. As we have seen from the work of Thomas Smith, this is not unusual in the work of amateur painters. The fact that Dummer was from twenty to twenty-five years younger than Thomas Smith may explain why his manner is less archaic. His painting resembles the period style of the Stuart Restoration very closely—at least as far as this can be judged from the *Selfportrait* and the *Portrait of His Wife*.

In view of Dummer's intimate knowledge of English silverware of the latest fashion, it is not surprising to find him just as well acquainted with the painting manners of London. The *Selfportrait* (Fig. 43) recalls Godfrey Kneller's condescending grace, the portrait of *Mrs. Anna Atwater Dummer* (Fig. 45) reminds one more

[19] *Limners and Likenesses, op. cit.*, p. 20.

of the sober and searching mood of Michael Dahl (Fig. 46). It has been suggested that the foreign influence came to him by way of mezzotint reproductions. I would rather think Dummer saw original canvases. Engravings could not show to him an effect which he was eager to emulate in his wife's likeness, namely, the combination of precise facial design and broad sketchy drapery. In England such an effect was sometimes accidentally caused by the collaboration of several painters on one and the same portrait—the master finishing the face, but leaving everything else to his numerous assistants: the drapery-man, the wig-man, the coat-painter, the face-painter, and so forth. Particularly in Kneller's studio were these methods "established upon as regular principles as the fabricating of carpets at Kidderminster."[20]

If we sum up what we have seen of seventeenth-century art in New England, all signs seem to indicate a progressive assimilation of the European tradition. The limners of the 'seventies were more or less ignorant of contemporary English art. The amateurs of the 'eighties and 'nineties began imitating it—old Thomas Smith less skillfully than young Dummer and less emancipated from the archaic style. One would expect that painters more docile would follow until the assimilation process was complete. However, the development did not take that course.

Perhaps colonial painting would have really become undistinguishably like its mother art on the other side of the Atlantic had it been determined exclusively by New England. But the development was determined quite as much by New Netherland. Only one root of the American tradition sprang from the Boston school. The other root sprang from the school of New York. It was to the credit of that Dutch center that the suave manner of Sir Godfrey Kneller was soon transformed into a more rough, burry idiom; in fact, something that foreshadowed the American cartoon.

[20]William T. Whitley, *Artists and Their Friends in England,* London, 1928, I, pp. 4 ff.

## VI. *Professional Painters from Overseas*

In Europe century-old stable traditions have so determined the art of regions and municipalities that to mention the Paris school, the Munich school, or the Glasgow school, means something very specific in each instance. In America it was different. Here the quicksand-like substructure of civilization, rapidly shifting with its advancing frontier, did not encourage the formation of local schools, either in the past or in the present. If we say "the Chicago school," we mean at best a group of artists swept into the city yesterday from the four corners of the continent and ready to disband to-morrow. "The itinerant" is a more meaningful symbol of American art than "the school."

Local schools with well-defined traditions came into being only at two places, and right in the beginning of the history of American art: the Boston school of which I have just spoken, and where the early limners, Jeremiah Dummer, John Smibert, Robert Feke, and John Copley were to form a steady line through about one hundred years; and the school of New York, the beginnings of which shall be discussed presently. Elsewhere in the colonies the intended organi-zations of local schools never got beyond the formative phase; as, for instance, in Philadelphia, though it was to have the earliest na-tional academy. The Boston and New York schools alone fashioned the American tradition and have remained to this day, despite all efforts toward decentralization, the dominant schools of the United States.

On the other hand, the American milieu possessed from the start a curious power of making over immigrants into Americans. Very few continued to paint in the New World exactly as they had painted in the Old, as did Henrietta Johnson, who came to the South around 1700, and John Watson (1684–1762), who came to Perth Amboy from Scotland in 1715.

Henrietta Johnson's suave little pastels were uniformly done in a manner reminiscent of her Italian contemporary, Rosalba Carriera.

All the ladies and gentlemen who sat for her look like members of one family, no matter whether the portrait was done in 1705 in South Carolina (*e.g., Sir Nathaniel Johnson*)[21] or in 1725 in New York (*e.g., Frances Moore,* owned by Mrs. Luke V. Lockwood, Stamford, Conn.).

Watson's painting of *Sir Peter Warren,* of 1731 (Thomas B. Clarke collection), and his little pen-and-ink likenesses are typical of an amateurish imitator of Kneller. And Dunlap's description of the painter's house, especially of its shutters adorned with heroes in antique costumes, leaves no doubt that Watson aped also the Franco-Italian fresco painters of the eighteenth-century London who used to apotheosize kings and generals in a similar allegorical masquerade.

Another such gentleman painter was Gustavus Hesselius (1682–1755), though he was decidedly of bigger caliber. He came from Dalecarlia, the central province of Sweden, where his ancestors both on his father's and his mother's side had long been known as distinguished scholars and clergymen; Emanuel Swedenborg was his cousin. Accompanying his brother, Andreas, who was called as pastor to New Sweden, Gustavus Hesselius landed on May 1, 1712, at Wilmington, Del. He married three years later, moved eventually to Annapolis, Md., and spent the last twelve years of his life in Philadelphia. He died at the age of seventy-three. A fuller story of his life has been recently published by Christian Brinton.[22]

Hesselius learned the painter's trade in Stockholm,[23] that is, in a school remarkable for its colorless internationalism. All the artists employed by Charles XI were foreigners, mostly German and Dutch of Italian training. The portraits as well as the historical and

[21]Robert Wilson: "Art and Artists in Provincial South Carolina" (*Charleston Year Book*), 1899.

[22]*Gustavus Hesselius, an Exhibition Held at the Philadelphia Museum of Art,* Philadelphia, 1938, pp. 7–18.

[23]"There is no trustworthy evidence that he ever travelled or studied on the continent" (C. Brinton, in his above mentioned *vita* of Hesselius). Rembrandt Peale's contention that Hesselius was a student of Kneller in London may be

mythological paintings of the late seventeenth and early eighteenth centuries in churches, royal castles and private homes in and around Stockholm could have been produced anywhere else in Europe; nothing distinguished them as Swedish. David Klöcker von Ehrenstrahl, who died when Hesselius was sixteen, and his nephew David von Krafft, who was most influential in Stockholm at the time of Hesselius' 'prenticeship, were skillful and thorough painters, but nothing beyond that.[24] The curious lack of any personal bias and conviction in their work seems to me characteristic also of Hesselius. His paintings represent the stock in trade of the periwig age. The easy way in which he changed his religious allegiance when it was opportune to do so is the cue to his painting. A Swedish Lutheran in New Sweden, a Church-of-England man in Maryland, a Moravian when he was commissioned to install a pipe organ in the church of the brotherhood at Bethlehem, Pa., and a Swedish Lutheran when his daughter married a pastor of that fold. Christian Brinton is right in adding: "Hesselius was as spiritually versatile as he was so in the æsthetic sense."

Hesselius' approach is best described by a phrase with which he recommended his services to the Philadelphians, "Painting done *in the best manner*[25]–he might as well have said "in the standard international manner." Small wonder that there is no trace of "development" apparent in his paintings, no progression in any definite direction. They are all solid likenesses. The painter did not flatter his sitters, but neither did he characterize them. *Mistress Galloway* of Tulip Hill, Md. (1721, Metropolitan Museum of Art), the first of his likenesses of which there is any specific record, and perhaps

---

due to a misunderstanding; occasionally Hesselius painted copies after Kneller. The Historical Society of Pennsylvania owns a copy of his after Kneller's *Margaret Penn Fream* (Cf. *Pennsylvania Magazine,* XXVIII, 1904, p. 36; and *Exhibition of American Portraits at the Academy of Fine Arts,* Philadelphia, 1934, pp. 68 ff.).

[24]See August Hahr: *David von Krafft och den Ehrenstrahlska skolan,* Uppsala, 1900.

[25]*Pennsylvania Gazette,* December 11, 1740.

his best one, too—who would guess that the old lady was in her ninetieth year when she posed for Hesselius? The *Robert Morris, Sr.* (*circa* 1748, Historical Society of Pennsylvania), a portrait of the same average quality—who, upon seeing the two pictures side by side, would conclude that the painter was thirty-nine when he did the one and sixty-six or older when he did the other?

## VII. *The Primitives of New York*

The new seeing is evident in the school of New York. This other root of the American tradition was an offshoot of the living growth of art in Protestant Holland. In contrast to New England, divorced as it was from Stuart England, New Netherland remained an integral part of the mother country. Back of the early portraits of New York was the tradition of the Amsterdam school of the early seventeenth century.

Contrary to the ostentatious court art of England and its ancestor, the Roman Catholic art of Flanders, Protestant Dutch art was always of and for the middle classes, concerned with what the burgher liked in life and admired in pictures. Dutch painting was at its best when it represented things and facts soberly, in dry pictorial prose. From the brothers van Eyck through Hugo van der Goes, Geertgen tot Sint Jans, and Jerome Bosch, to Thomas de Kejzer and the young Rembrandt, its special domain was still-life, likenesses, and genre pictures—the kind that, like stock-taking, requires conscientious painstaking description and admits of only a moderate departure from the factual—more readily in the service of caricature than of idealization. The rational, slightly primitive, mind of middle-class men appreciates that sort of thing in a likeness more than flattery.

Dutch art was fundamentally unromantic. At times its sobriety developed into an austere simplicity which reminds one, especially as regards pictorial construction, of early Grecian art.[26] The clair-

[26]How closely the pictorial composition of Frans Hals approximated the archaic art of Greece has recently been pointed out by Willi Drost: *Barockmalerei in den germanischen Ländern*, Wildpark-Potsdam, 1926, pp. 144 ff.

ɔbscure painting of Holland in particular, was consistent with the lispassionate temper of businessmen and the scholar's regard for neticulous workmanship. Diametrically different from the exuberınt colorism of Rubens and van Dyck, the Dutch clair-obscure ɔainters subordinated all colors to a universal tone until the separate ints, deprived of their chromatic brilliance, were reduced to mere 'values" in a bright drabness—witness, the pictures of Thomas de Kejzer, Govert Flink, Ferdinand Bol, and Rembrandt until the ixteen-hundred-and-forties.

The earliest limners of New Amsterdam came from that school, even though not all of them were actually "trained" therein. Several ɔainters can be identified. The Duyckinck family extended through nore than a century. Their ancestral head, Evert Duyckinck I (1621–1702), came in 1638, opened a glazier's shop and henceorth was mentioned as a glassmaker, limner and painter. A porrait of *Stephanus van Cortland,* painted by him in 1693, was shown ıt the Century Association of New York in 1925. He was the first New Yorker who extended his sphere of activity to Boston, provided he likeness of *Lt.-Governor William Stoughton,* in the Boston Athenæum, is rightly attributed to him. In 1679, when Evert I was naking and painting the glass for a new church, his son Gerret (1660–*circa* 1710) was "doing most of the work," and was already eaching drawing, for instance to his brother-in-law, Jaspar Denkers. In 1699, this second Duyckinck painted the portrait of Mayor van Cortland's daughter *Ann (de Lancey)*. Gerret's oldest son, Evert III (1677–1727), is but vaguely known as a limner from a ɔortrait of *Ann Sinclair Crommelin,* dated 1725. Gerret's other son, Gerardus Duyckinck (1695–1742), was the last of the dynasty. His ɔortrait of *Chief Justice, Lt.-Governor James de Lancey,* is dated 1728.

Jacobus Gerritsen Strijker (d. 1687), probably the most distinguished painter of early New York, belonged to another prominent New Amsterdam family. He was born in the Dutch province of Drente and crossed the sea in 1651 as "a man of considerable means and decided culture." Three of his portraits are known. The one of his brother, *Jan Strijker* (dated 1655, Thomas B. Clarke Collection), was preserved as a sacred relic in the family ever since the artist solemnly dedicated it to his daughter Altje. The tradition that Strijker was Rembrandt's personal student in Amsterdam is supported, however vaguely, by the maiden name of his Dutch wife, Ytie Huibrechts. Huibrechts was also the maiden name of the mother-in-law of Titus van Rhijn, Rembrandt's son and pupil.

From the early pictures that have survived it can barely be surmised to what extent Dutch painting was imitated in New Amsterdam. By the end of the seventeenth century, when examples become more numerous, the Dutch tradition had already been reduced to an archaic New York manner.

As in Boston, the limner's experience may have been partly responsible for this crude reduction. On the other hand, the New Yorkers adapted the Dutch style to their particular wants. And they were more intimately familiar with the Dutch than the Bostonians were with the British. Instead of emulating Rembrandt, as Dummer emulated Kneller and Dahl, the painters of New York translated the polished Dutch speech into a homely colonial idiom which the New Yorkers more readily appreciated. In other words, theirs was a straight secession, caused probably by the realization that the fineries of the Old World were unsuited to the new environment. Something so constructive cannot be explained from mere technical inefficiency on the part of the painters. A new goal was pursued. Another will was at work.

Gerret Duyckinck's *Portrait of His Wife* (*ante* 1710, New York Historical Society, Fig. 50) illustrates the stylistic transformation to best advantage. Its arrangement—half-length, turned slightly to the spectator's left, one hand reposing on the bosom—relies, probably indirectly, on the authority of certain Dutch prototypes, notably of Rembrandt's early or middle periods, such as *Saskia van Uylenburg,* of 1643 (Berlin, Kaiser Friedrich Museum, Fig. 48). A comparison reveals in what measure the Dutch mellow-hued atmospheric envelope was drained off by Duyckinck. The sitter is not embedded in glowing light-dark. Rembrandt's liquid forms, fairly bathed in iridescent clair-obscure, have been superseded by implastic forms, hard angular lines, and plain, neutrally lighted, unbroken surfaces. Eyebrow and nose, as in Thomas Smith's portrait of his daughter *Maria Catherine* (Fig. 42), are bordered by a single flat dark arch.

Art historians are well acquainted from past epochs with analogous transmutations of style. They occurred inevitably whenever archaic civilizations departed from mother civilizations that had grown overripe. Substitution of a manner pliant and rich by one rigid and wanting in variety occurred, for example, on the verge of the ancient Roman and early Christian epochs. Roman portraits painted when the empire was still on its cultural crest bore all the hallmarks of objective naturalism (Fig. 47). One hundred and fifty years later, however, in the formative phase of Christianization, elaborate modelling, color hues, and atmospheric lighting of the ancient style were reduced to something not liquid, a crude manner of painting in terms of inflexible planes and lines stripped of atmosphere. (Fig. 49). It is not an accidental coincidence that colonial archaism seceded from the old-world baroque exactly at the moment when the colonists were deserting the old civilization in search of another more primitive one. The atavistic process of archaization attendant on the formation of a distinctly native tradition should reconcile us with certain oddities in the art of the early limners. It should make it easier for us to give them the credit they deserve for discarding methods of painting which were unfit for the colonial temper, and for creating formulæ simple and workable enough as starting points for a new American art.

Incidentally, let us clear away a very common misunderstanding about limners such as Evert Duyckinck III and Pieter Vanderlyn, whose likenesses are sometimes dismissed as something too bungling to qualify as art at all. The limners of New York, like all other archaic artists, were not so much "bunglers" as "expressionists."

Expressionists often seem awkward because their pictorial statements are partial and, therefore, overemphatic. The classical Dutch painters, from whom the New York limners seceded, never overemphasized anything. Endeavoring to do full "justice" to their sitters, they painted the objective truth *sine ira cum studio*. Their followers in America, being more subjective and therefore less "just," overemphasized line at the expense of atmospheric chiaroscuro and ugliness at the expense of normal characterization. Some of them substituted caricature for characterization. Certainly none of the New Yorkers did what Hogarth afterwards ironically advised English portraitists to do: "Whoever would succeed in this branch must adopt the mode recommended in one of Gay's fables, and make divinities of all who sit to him."

Heads earthy and full of character, but unsightly in an appalling measure, such as *Mrs. Thomas van Alstyne* (1721, New York Historical Society, Fig. 51), by the Dutch-born Pieter Vanderlyn (1682–1778), bear all the earmarks of archaic overstress, something that is common only in periods when artists were either so obtuse that they could not distinguish the sublime from the ridiculous or so oppressed that they could not muster the good humor that is needed to say the ridiculous frankly and have a good time with it. In what measure these primitives were sometimes uncritical of their own gross mistakes may be seen from the left arm and its flower-bearing hand, posed in the fashionable manner of Caspar Netcher.[27] The hand is sadly misrepresented. In the position in which it is supposed to be the thumb and index finger of a *left* hand would not appear in front, but in back, of the fingers. What Vanderlyn drew would be correct if it were the lady's *right* hand brought over to her left side by moving the right upper arm athwart the body. Artist and patroness do not seem to have minded. The error was never corrected and the painter was allowed to paint *Mr. Thomas van Alstyne* as a companion picture.

[27]Compare, for instance, C. Netcher's *Lady with an Orange,* of 1681, No. 167 of the Wallace Collection, London.

Heads represented with an almost brutal partiality, such as *Reverend Thomas Thacher* (Boston, Old North Church, Fig. 52) and *Ann Pollard* (1721, Mass. Historical Society, Fig. 53), would by rights have to be attributed to some unknown New Englander. However, in a period when itinerant painters were grazing every corner of the country for patrons, the domicile of the models is no sound criterion. These caricatures were polar opposites to the reticent, non-expressionist Massachusetts taste of the closing seventeenth century. Moreover, the portrait of *Ann Pollard* is a clear echo, colonialized of course, of certain well-known Dutch prototypes. It may remotely remind one-time visitors to the Rijksmuseum of Amsterdam of certain pictures of hard-featured old ladies, such as Ferdinand Bol's *Elizabeth Bas,* or groups of them in the *Spinhuis* likenesses of Dirk Santvoort. Incidentally, the limner who painted *Ann Pollard* must have been a singularly twisted fellow. From the manner in which he fashioned the kerchief over the old lady's chest, like the stern frame of a galley, I could imagine him to have been a shipwright, a member of that honorable trade from which were soon to come our earliest carvers of figureheads for ships and, eventually, our earliest sculptor, William Rush.

At all events, the unknown authors of these last-named portraits were obviously not reared in or near Boston where a more conservative adherence to the niceties of British taste was manifest in many ways then as well as later. Only five years after the completion of the *Ann Pollard* picture the English mezzotinter Peter Pelham settled in Boston, and after only eight years John Smibert, a Scotch painter, British and Italian trained, was given the opportunity of staging the first art exhibition in the New World, an exhibition of pure European traditions in which the Bostonians found commendable all that the school of New York shunned:

*'Tis yours, Great Master, in just lines to trace*
*The rising Prospect, or the lovely Face.*
*In the fair Round to swell the glowing cheek,*
*Give Thought to Shades, and bid the Colours speak.*

## CHAPTER TWO

# JOHN SMIBERT

### I. *Smibert in England and Italy*

JOHN SMIBERT AND ROBERT FEKE, the first clearly perceptible characters in the history of early colonial art, stand forth today like two lone posts left standing in the debris of an old homestead. It is the duty of American archeology to ascertain their significance. For, without a clear conception of the functions of these two, the whole structure of colonial art is likely to be misinterpreted. Historians are agreed that colonial painting pivoted on them. But apparently they do not agree on their respective significance.

With Smibert and Feke we encounter for the first time the opposition of English and American training, a phenomenon which we shall meet again and again in the history of American art, and which is peculiar to America; at least I know of nothing similar in Europe. We shall find it in the middle colonial period with Benjamin West and Copley; in the late colonial period with Gilbert Stuart and John Trumbull; before the Civil War with Thomas Cole and Asher Brown Durand; during and after the Civil War with James Whistler and Winslow Homer; and so on for later generations. In every period new-country views upheld by one leading artist conflicted with the old-country views held by another. And, with one or the other trend preponderant at different times, this periodical conflict of traditions functioned like the current and the countercurrent in the permanent stream of the development.

Naturally, greater significance should be attributed to Robert Feke, the native American, than to John Smibert, a Scotsman trained in England who did not come to Rhode Island until he had reached the age of forty, when his style was set in the old-country tradition.[1]

In Edinburgh, where he was born, John Smibert was trained as an artisan. He did not receive the education of an artist that some of his young friends received in the studio of Sir John Medina. He was apprenticed to an unknown local house painter and plasterer and served his master for seven years before going to London. There, for many years, it did not enter his head that he might become an artist. "In all that time he had a strong inclination to drawing and studying, but no opportunity to improve," says the antiquarian George Vertue, who gives one the impression that his friend Smibert drifted by accident into the painter's career. Odd jobs for an art dealer in London, including occasional copies from old pictures, may have familiarized young Smibert with the elements of oil painting. But from ten to twelve years elapsed before he worked "either from life or from casts."

At long last Smibert entered the academy. This must have been before he went to Italy in 1717 when the only academy in London was the one on Great Queen Street; James Thornhill had been its governor since 1716. At that time Thornhill was painting frescoes in an Italian taste, decorations of the cupola of St. Paul's Cathedral and of the "Painted Hall" at Greenwich. It is quite possible that Smibert, employed in doing the plastering for Thornhill's frescoes, attracted the distinguished master's attention by an occasional

[1]Alan Burroughs, *Limners and Likenesses, op. cit.*, sees it the other way. Irrespective of the facts that Smibert came at forty and had not seen a scrap of colonial painting before disembarking on the new shore, the Scotsman is introduced as the representative *American* painter. Feke, the native of Oyster Bay, L. I., who grew up under the direct influence of the school of New York, is described as the typical *British* artist: "Smibert's bluntness is characteristic of the most original work done in America . . . before and after this time. Feke's formal charm is characteristic of aristocratic English portraiture" (p. 47). This theory appears unsound in the light of the biographical data and untenable in the light of the stylistic idiosyncrasies of the two painters. All that is needed to clear the argument is, I believe, a fuller presentation of the case of Smibert and the case of Feke, such as I am giving above.

manifestation of artistic skill and that, on the strength of this, he was admitted to the academy's school. For the tradition that Smibert studied at the "Academy of Sir James Thornhill" can only refer to the Great Queen Street Academy at the time of Thornhill's governorship. The institution at Coventgarden which was afterwards known as "Sir James Thornhill's Academy" did not open until the year when Smibert returned from Italy. I am saying this emphatically because confusion of the two academies has entailed a number of errors, the worst of which pertains to the supposed friendship of Smibert and Hogarth.

For one thing, they were not fellow students at the academy. At the time of Smibert's Italian journey, Hogarth was still engraving business cards, family crests, and, eventually, book plates as 'prentice in the shop of silversmith Ellis Gamble. Hogarth did not even plan to be a painter until Smibert was back in England and the academy in which he enrolled in 1720 was the "Academy at St. Martin's Lane," a school conducted by Thornhill's opponents, Cheron and Vanderbanck.

In their endeavors to link Smibert with Hogarth, critics have been led farther astray by spurious evidence. In John Smibert's *vita* in the *Dictionary of National Biography* an engraving after a portrait of the poet *Allan Ramsay* is mentioned which is supposed to bear the inscription "by John Smibert, *the Scottish Hogarth.*" Theodore Bolton took this reference to "indicate both some fame on Smibert's part as well as suggesting a possible friendship with Hogarth."[2] The portrait in question (Fig. 2) forms the frontispiece of Allan Ramsay's Poems of 1721.[3] It bears the initials of John Smibert, the painter,[4] and T. Vercruysse,[5] the engraver. But there

[2]*Fine Arts,* August, 1935, p. 12.

[3]Poems by Allan Ramsay, Edinburgh: printed by Mr. Thomas Ruddiman, for the author, 1721.

[4]Smibert subscribed to the book of his fellow townsman. It is noteworthy that in the long "Alphabetical List of such of the subscribers' names as have come to hand," comprising dukes, lords, earls, baronets, professors, merchants, writers, and booksellers, Smibert is mentioned on p. xxviii as the only *painter.*

[5]Vercruysse was active in Florence at the time of Smibert's sojourn there.

is no reference to a *Scottish Hogarth.* Of course not. The phrase would have made no sense in 1721; Hogarth's earliest portraits came in the seventeen-hundred-and-thirties.

The chronology of Smibert's early life arranges itself, if 1716, the probable year of his admission to the Academy under James Thornhill's governorship, is taken as *point fixe,* and the years that Vertue furnishes in his biographical sketch are counted backward. Three to four years before entering the academy (four seem more likely than three in consideration of his having first worked as a coach painter) set Smibert's arrival in London at 1712. Seven previous years in Edinburgh in the service of the master plasterer establish 1705 as the beginning of his career. Two further years, which should be allowed for 'prenticeship, suggest 1703 as the time when he left school. He was fifteen then—the average age for a youngster to start working for his own living.

Late in 1717 Smibert set out for Italy.[6] The itinerary, *Florence, Rome, Naples, etc.,* as given by Vertue, suggests the Grand Tour of an ambitious young painter who wanted to perfect his academic education by seeing the continent, visiting famous artists and art collections, and copying the old masters. Coming from a one-time plasterer, the plan of three years abroad leaves little doubt that Smibert was hoping for a better future than fate had in store for him. The tour would have been out of all proportion had he planned to become a simple face painter; but it was well-planned if he was expecting to paint frescoes of the kind that were reaping fame and fortune for James Thornhill and many another of the London painters native and foreign.

For by the time Smibert entered the academy at Great Queen Street, London had become the haunt of Italian and French muralists. The capital was soon to be a city of academies and the era of the portrait shops was ending. The peerage were having their palaces decorated to rival Versailles and Vienna. Antonio Verrio,

[6]Before sailing, Smibert visited Edinburgh; a portrait, dated 1717, is owned by Lady Grant, Monymusk Castle, Scotland.

the decorator of Windsor Castle and Hampton Court, died, and Giovanni Antonio Pellegrini left, before Smibert first came to London. But Sebastiano Ricci, who had recently completed the frescoes at Schönbrunn, remained in London until 1716 together with his nephew Marco. Under Smibert's very eyes the Riccis were setting up examples of the extravagant Venetian baroque—in Burlington House, in the palace of the Duke of Montagu, in the Duke of Portland's chapel at Bulstrode, and in Chelsea Hospital. When they returned to the continent, Antonio Bellucci took their place. Within a short while the Italian vogue became such a menace to British-born artists that Lord Halifax, nationally minded as he was, used his influence so that Englishmen were given commissions too; for instance Thornhill.

In these circumstances Smibert would have found Venice a better place for study than Florence. Nevertheless, there were some new frescoes worth seeing even in Florence. The ceiling of the Grand Hall of the Palazzo Riccardi, painted by the facile Luca Giordano with a huge Apotheosis of the Medici dynasty, resembled somewhat Thornhill's Apotheosis of William and Mary in the Painted Hall at Greenwich. At places south of Florence there were many other recent fresco decorations to interest English artists, painted by Francesco Solimena, Baciccio, and Pozzo; the former two were living, the latter had died recently.

Unfortunately no evidence of Smibert's timely interest in fresco painting has survived. Vertue mentioned only that Smibert painted "heads" in Italy, but he was surely insufficiently informed on saying that Smibert made that "his whole study." He painted replicas of old master's tableaux. Moreover, before he came to America—not only toward the end of his life "when his eyesight was failing" —Smibert painted "landskips."

This fact is put beyond doubt by the poem of an unidentifie[d] admirer written in Boston for the occasion of an exhibition [of] Smibert's original paintings and replicas, an undertaking designe[d] to recommend the painter's services to the Bostonians three month[s] after his arrival. The poem, a versified catalogue of that memorable art show—the first ever held in America—gives quite a clear idea of what most impressed Smibert on his Italian trip.[7] It enumerates a few portraits of ladies, giving their names in Latin—for propriety's ake, I suppose—a few male portraits that still exist[8] and Smibert's eplicas after Rubens, van Dyck, and "the Italian Master" (either Raphael or Titian). Casts of the Venus Medici and the Head of Homer, known to have been the artist's prize possessions, are eferred to as "The breathing Statue and the living Bust."

Smibert's visit to Italy, it should be remembered, fell in a period when everybody was collecting archeological curios on a large scale. Pope Clement XI and his Cardinals were outdoing each other in scouring every corner of Rome for ancient marbles and bronzes. Foreign princes employed agents. Even the untitled were assembling what their more limited means would buy in the way of seals, intaglios, and pastes.

The collecting of art works had always been the pride and passion of the Medici; the tradition of Lorenzo Magnifico, whose "garden of antiquities" once had been an *haute école* to Michelangelo, was till upheld by the last Grand Duke. In Smibert's days a greater quantity of art works were assembled in their collections than ever before. The mind of Cosimo III was on matters of the Church more han the arts. Nevertheless, it was he who centralized in Florence he once widely scattered treasures of the family, including those of the Villa Medici of Rome. Some of the canvases that Smibert copied were in the Uffizi, where Copley saw them in 1775 and felt at once reminded of the replicas then in Boston. In the Tribuna was Raphael's *Madonna dell' Impannata,*[9] Titian's *Venus and*

[7]The poem, preserved in the *London Daily Courant* of April, 1730, has been blished by Henry Wilder Foote: "Mr. Smibert shows his pictures. March 30," in *The New England Quarterly,* Vol. VIII (March–December, 1935), . 14 ff.

[8]*Viz.,* Chief Justice Sewall, Nathaniel Byfield, General Mascarene.

[9]This is the only painting in the Medici collections that fits Copley's description of Smibert's copy of "a holy family by Raphael."

*Cupid* hung in an adjoining hall. These pictures were accessible to any student. But van Dyck's *Cardinal Bentivoglio* was in the Grand Duke's private quarters in the Pitti Palace. It was an unusual privilege that Smibert was allowed to copy a part of this picture. Was it out of fond recollections of England that the old tyrant admitted Smibert to his sanctum? He had visited England in the days of Charles II and had posed for Samuel Cooper at that time.[10]

Some of Smibert's replicas have survived. The head of *Cardinal Bentivoglio* is at Harvard (Fig. 54). *The Continence of Scipio* after Poussin, is perhaps identical with a painting in the Walker Art Gallery of Bowdoin College.[11] The bulk of the collection was exhibited in Smibert's home before 1735.[12] Doctor Alexander Hamilton, a Scotch physician, visiting there in 1745, mentioned among the reproductions of ancient sculptures that he particularly admired *Homer's Head* and *The Venus of Medicis*.[13] The remark of the keeper of Smibert's estate, made to Charles Wilson Peale sever

[10]*Travels of Cosmo III, Grand Duke of Tuscany, through England,* translated from the Italian MS in the Laurentian Library at Florence; London 1821, pp. 343 ff. and 346 f. The narrator of these travels was Count Lorenzo Magalotti.

[11]Doctor Alexander Hamilton saw the picture in July, 1745, as part of "a fine collection of pictures, good busts and statues, most of them antiques, some in clay and paste," and described it as "that part of Scipio's history in Spain where he delivers the lady to the prince to whome she had been betrothed." Copley commented at length on the *Sippeo,* in a letter from Paris (*Copley Pelham Letters, loc. cit.,* September, 1774). It was greatly admired by John Trumbull when he rented Smibert's vacant studio in 1821. The painting at Bowdoin College (No. 132) was adjudged by Gilbert Stuart "a first rate copy."

[12]In that year Bishop Berkeley, in a letter from Ireland, tried to persuade Smibert "to embark with your busts, your prints, and your drawings, and once more cross the Atlantic."

[13]Doctor Alexander Hamilton's *Itinerarium* (privately printed at St. Louis) 1907.—It must have been from Smibert's cast that Copley, at the age of nineteen, drew the Venus Medici, with measurements added, in his sketchbook with anatomical studies (British Museum). From two other drawings (*ibid.,* pp. 4 6) I would infer that Smibert also had a cast of the Laocoön group.

years after his master's death, that he "spent a fortune in Italy," was well founded.[14]

According to the "versified catalogue," Smibert's art exhibition of 1730 included picturesque "landscapes of mood":

> *Roman ruins nod their awful heads . . .*
>
> . . . . . . . . . .
>
> *Landscapes, how gay! arise in ev'ry light . . .*
>
> . . . . . . . . . .
>
> *Thro' Fairy scenes the roving Fancy strays*
> *Lost in the endless visionary maze . . .*
>
> . . . . . . . . . .
>
> *The same gay scene our beauteous works adorn*
> *The flaming Evening or the Rosy Morn.*

Pictures of ancient ruins inviting the beholder's fancy to roam through their endless maze and to be moved to tears by their sentimental illumination—that particular class of painting was becoming fashionable when Smibert visited Italy and was the rage in England when he left for America. What was shown at Boston may have been in the nature of Giovanni Paolo Panini's *Antiquities* (engravings of which Smibert ordered from Arthur Pond in London by the dozen in 1741), but it cannot have been Panini's work. Panini was a beginner when Smibert was in Italy and the very earliest of his *ancient ruins* dates from 1727. It might have been replicas after Marco Ricci, painted in London, or it might have been replicas after Alessandro Magnasco from whom Ricci derived his inspiration. Another painting in the show was certainly after Magnasco; the very subject gives its author away—the versified catalogue refers to it as *Gloating Monks.* Magnasco was in the employ of the Medici when Smibert was in Florence.[15]

[14]The remark was recorded by Charles W. Peale in a letter to his son, quoted in John Sartain's *Reminiscences of a very Old Man.*

[15]Smibert's association with Magnasco clears away the last doubt as to when exactly Magnasco entered the service of the Medici court. According to his

Alessandro Magnasco, nicknamed Lissandrino because of hi small stature, was a romantic *par excellence*. His mercurial minc was obsessed with everything that is weird and demoniac and hi picturesque manner was a perfect vehicle for that mind. Magnasco' favorite form of expression was sketches painted with angular jerk of the brush in a sort of shorthand notation. His subjects were o the kind that critics of the eighteenth century classified as "ex tremely picturesque." In his landscapes and seascapes, earth anc water were but instruments to him—organs, as it were, on whicl he rhapsodized on visionary themes, whether it be ships tossec sky-high by mountainous waves or wind-ridden wildernesses witl jagged trees writhing under storm-cleft clouds. He loved to pain darkness lurking in unexplained corners; crumbling walls, arche and columns; gnarled roots and knotted tree trunks. In figure piece his passion was for weird folk-scenes—minstrels grinding the barre organ to old hags and beggars, episodes of inquisition and torture and, above all, the lurid mysteries of monastic life: wild-eyec monks whipping their own bare flesh to shreds, or staring into spac in silent meditation. Those themes were Magnasco's monopoly Wherever a picture of "gloating monks" is mentioned in an eigh teenth-century exhibition, it is a safe guess that Magnasco wa its author.

His interpretation always had a touch of caricature. Protestant minds, in particular, were bound to read satirical innuendo intc Magnasco's ghostly illumination, his distorted design and the chapped and cloven manner of his brushwork. At all events, we may

---

biographer, Carlo Giuseppe Ratti, the Genoese was employed by Cosimo III' son, Gian Gastone. But inasmuch as Gian Gastone did not accede until 172 when Magnasco was fifty-six, and since such a late visit to Florence is out o keeping with what is otherwise known of the painter's life, historians now agre that Magnasco was painter to the hereditary prince when the old Grand Duk was still the sovereign. Ratti says that Magnasco's sojourn in Florence was o long duration, but critics have as yet been unable to ascertain when it began His association with Smibert, who was in Florence between 1717 and 1720 should prove that Magnasco was in Florence before 1720.

rest assured that the unknown versifier of 1730 did not rejoice for æsthetic reasons. His, and probably Smibert's, admiration for "the gloating monks" was pure glee over so sarcastic a condemnation of popery where it was shown at its worst.[16]

Another more important bit of evidence of Smibert's acquaintance with Magnasco is the *Pencil Portrait of Grand Duke Cosimo III* in the Walker Art Building of Bowdoin College in Brunswick, Me. (Fig. 55). The drawing betrays the stylistic marks of Magnasco's hand, but it is attributed to Smibert on the evidence of a legend written beneath the head on another bond paper and in early nineteenth-century script as follows: *Cosmo the 3rd, Grand Duke of Tuscany, from the life, by John Smibert.*[17] The artistic "handwriting" of Smibert is not well documented prior to 1728 and it may very well have changed considerably over a lapse of eleven years. But even if this is taken into account, one thing should be certain: The eye and mind that perceived the bigoted, imbecile, old Grand Duke in terms of such a daring caricature cannot be identical with the mind and eye that fashioned the bluntly drawn early likenesses in Scotland or the sober heads of New England worthies which are incontestably Smibert's later work. It is difficult to believe that Smibert ever drew like Magnasco, unless he

[16]Considering that the other replicas and casts of Smibert's collection all stemmed from works in the collection of the Grand Duke of Tuscany, it is almost certain that the copy after Magnasco was also from a work in the Pitti Palace. One of two that hung on the ground floor is now in the Uffizi (No. 1048). Its title, *Landscape with Monks in Prayer,* fits the description *Gloating Monks* better than the other one which hung near it and is now No. 207 of the Pinacoteca of Turin, namely, *Landscape with Voyaging Monks.*

[17]The drawing is mounted on a sheet of paper different in texture from the drawing-paper and bearing the watermark of a Spanish (?) firm, VILLAREDA Y . . . I am indebted to Mr. Philip C. Beam, Assistant Director and Curator of The Walker Art Building, for the following information concerning the history of the drawing: "It was purchased, along with others now comprising the 'Bowdoin Drawings' here, in France by the Hon. James Bowdoin II during the reign of Napoleon. He brought the collection to this country on his return in 1809 and, on his death, the drawings came to the College by gift. That was in 1813."

tried to make a line-for-line copy of one of his drawings. And that may explain the mystery. The Bowdoin drawing is, I believe, a copy by Smibert after an original Magnasco.

The Bowdoin drawing has been examined by so few critics and so little of expert opinion has been voiced on it that I must ask the reader's patience while I present the case.

By 1809, when the drawing was purchased in France by James Bowdoin, Magnasco's name had fallen into oblivion[18] and Smibert's would surely not have been mentioned unless his name was on the drawing. I am unwilling to believe that the Scot said his drawing was "from the life" if it was a replica from another artist's picture. I would rather believe that what was written on the original margin (which was eventually trimmed off) was something like this: "after a drawing of Magnasco from the life . . ." After trimming the damaged margin, the later owner copied the legend, but omitted the words "after a drawing of Magnasco"; the unfamiliar artist and the fact itself were irrelevant to him.

Carlo Ratti speaks at length of Magnasco's portraits. A few of his painted portraits have been discovered recently but no portrait drawings of his have survived. It is quite difficult therefore to produce stylistic evidence that convinces any layman that Smibert copied an original likeness by Magnasco. Experts, conversant from Magnasco's other drawings with his peculiarly nervous sketchy and jerky manner *con brevi colpi di tocco di modo che paion fatti per disprezzo* (which, as Ratti says, was the same in his drawings and paintings), will no doubt recognize it in the Bowdoin drawing. Magnasco's characteristic linework is apparent at the throat, the lower lip, and the nose. The head (Fig. 56) from Magnasco's *Music Lesson,* even though it is no portrait, will, I trust, demonstrate the similarity of style. Compare the mannerisms that appear

[18]Benno Geiger, *Alessandro Magnasco* (Vienna, 1923), pp. 13 ff., points out that most of Magnasco's authentic paintings were catalogued at that time under the name of other painters, such as Rosa, Tempesta, Bassano, Bernazzano, Courtois, Callot, Goya, Alfano de Gomez, El Greco, *et al.*

in both the drawing and the painting: the thick lips of the open mouths and the nearly straight line denoting the nostrils. At this point, however, it may be seen that the Bowdoin drawing is a copy rather than an original. In the drawing, the horizontal line above the nostril has been entered falteringly; it is drawn without the authenticity and assuredness from which the corresponding line of the brush flowed in the painted head of the musician. And many other differences indicate that we are dealing with a replica. Even though the original is lost, one may be certain that its background was not shaded with boresome and petty cross-hatchings; Magnasco used to suggest a background with a few rubs of the fingertips. Smibert, however, in accordance with his taste for neat elaboration, changed the original sketch into a more "finished" picture, by completing it—even as he encircled the whole with a nice oval after the fashion of Godfrey Kneller. Smibert used such oval shapes for bust portraits until his dying day.

While all this may be said with a good deal of assurance, nothing better than guesswork can tell how the drawing got to France. Still, the history of the Medici, as recorded by G. F. Young, allows at least an hypothetical answer, and that corroborates my conjecture. The Grand Duchess of Tuscany, Marguerite of Orleans, living at Paris at the convent of Montmartre from 1676 to her death in 1721, used to amuse her royal cousin, Louis XIV of France, with funny reports on the latest imbecilities of Cosimo, her estranged husband. It is quite possible that a "cartoon" of Cosimo was included in one of the letters on which her *chronique scandaleuse* was founded. Most of these letters came to her from her son, Prince Gian Gastone, who was, as we remember, the employer of Magnasco. If Gian Gastone sent his mother a caricature of the old man whom they both detested and ridiculed, it would most likely have been drawn by Magnasco, the Prince's sergeant painter. Moreover, if the Prince enclosed a replica, instead of the original with which he did not wish to part, it was likely to be done by an obliging Mr. Smibert who happened to be in Florence at the time.

## II. *Smibert in New England*

From Italy Smibert returned to England in the company of the Reverend Doctor George Berkeley, Dean of Derry. The Dean was accompanying the son of the Bishop of Cloyne on his Grand Tour of the continent. In Florence they met John Smibert. The three stayed together and returned together. The Dean had an Utopian plan. He was going to found a college for Indian missionaries in Bermuda. The idea did not take shape until 1724, but it may have been a topic for conversation in Florence. "In his benevolent project for spreading knowledge in America," William Dunlap wrote "Berkeley did not neglect the important agency of the arts of design and having experience of the character and talents of Smibert, chose him as professor of drawing, painting, and architecture at his intended institution."[19] By the end of 1728 the great adventure got under way. In January, 1729, Dean Berkeley and his party, including the art professor elect, landed at Newport, R. I. The Dean bought a farm and awaited the funds promised him by the British government. But no funds were forthcoming. Smibert soon tired of waiting. Before the year was over he had moved to Boston. In the early spring of 1730 he held his art exhibition. In the fall he married Mary Williams, daughter of a local physician and schoolmaster. Soon thereafter he opened an art store at his house in Queen Street. He was settled in Boston for good.

The Dean was still waiting. After three years of waiting he returned to Ireland as Bishop of Cloyne.

Why did John Smibert give up civilized life in London for an uncertain existence in the town of Boston? Surely it was not for such a provincial future that he spent a fortune in Italy. If he went to America because he could not resist the persuasive personality of Berkeley, why did he stay when his protector returned home, prom-

[19]William Dunlap's *History of the Rise and Progress of the Arts of Design in the United States* (1834); new edition with additions by Frank W. Bayley and Charles E. Goodspeed, Boston, 1918, I, p. 23.

ising heaven on earth if Smibert would only follow?—a trading city four times as populous as Boston and a hundred times as rich; innumerable patrons and nobody else around to paint their likenesses; payment in gold instead of paper; a climate "where myrtles grow, without Boston pots, stoves, or greenhouses, in the open air."[20] Why did Smibert not listen to reason?

Contemporary comments leave a choice between two possible answers. Walpole says that disgust with the finesse of some of his profession and the promised tranquillity and honest subsistence in a healthy Elysian climate prompted the painter to turn his back on Europe; in other words, a loss of faith in "what Europe breeds n her decay" and absolute confidence in the paradise promised by Berkeley,

> *In happy climes, the seat of innocence,*
> *Where nature guides and virtue rules;*
> *Where men shall not impose for truth and sense*
> *The pedantry of courts and schools.*

Vertue, on the other hand, blames Smibert's departure on the artist's frustrated vanity. "He was not contented to be on a level with some of the lesser painters, but desired to be where he might be looked on at the top of his profession—then and thereafter."

The truth probably lies midway between these conflicting opinions. The reason Vertue gives is at variance with Walpole's description of Smibert as "a modest man." Vanity is a strong word; perhaps what Vertue meant was ambition—frustrated ambition. One cannot be at once vain and modest, but one can be modest in regard to his talents and ambitious to put them to better use. John Smibert was ambitious. A man with "a strong inclination for art" who after many years of drudgery climbs from plasterer to picture-restorer and academy student; spends three years of post-graduate study in Italy; enlists the protection of the Grand Duke of Tuscany -such a man is ambitious, no matter how modestly he may appraise

[20]William T. Whitley, *op. cit.,* I, p. 63.

his talents. Moreover, Walpole adds that Smibert was "silent." He did not talk about his art; perhaps out of an innate aversion to fighting. Now, if an artist ambitious but unable to "sell himself" and, in addition, disinclined to compete with rivals, is offered a position as head of an art school in some rival-proof elysium—will he not jump at the chance? Will he return, even at a friend's beckoning, after he is comfortably settled and is doing more business than he could hope to do in Ireland, where he would have to start all over again and against heavy competition? In Boston Smibert was "at the top of his profession." There his European training counted for immeasurably more than it did in England. In England nobody would have hailed a second-rater a "great master," as did the rimester of Boston.

The portrait of *Dean Berkeley* in the National Portrait Gallery of London, painted in 1728 before the artist sailed to the New World, proves that Smibert was a second-rater from the start and did not deteriorate into one in America. Moreover, it is only fair to say that he tried at first to adjust his manner of painting to the taste of his colonial customers. Only after about a dozen years did he fall back from honest characterization to superficial British mannerisms. The chronology of his dated half-lengths and quarter-lengths demonstrates that change with all desirable clearness.

Regard, for example, the portrait of *Nathaniel Byfield* (1730, Metropolitan Museum, Fig. 57). Even if one reckons with the possible influence of Peter Pelham's portrait engravings, the realistic characterization is astonishing for a one-time student of James Thornhill and one who copied van Dyck's *Cardinal Bentivoglio*. But after about ten years the painter's style slid back into that polite gentility which we are wont to associate with the British school rather than with the colonial. *Benjamin Pratt* (1741, Harvard University, Fig. 58) was perhaps no less "faithful" a likeness, but one much more bland and polished. Of course the different physiognomies of the sitters must be borne in mind. Byfield was a plain, toothless, obese old gentleman; Pratt was a younger man, slender-faced, wakeful and good-looking. Still, the change of approach is obvious. To mention one thing, the proportions are different. *Nathaniel Byfield* was viewed from in front after the primitive fashion and was somewhat cramped by the oval frame. *Benjamin Pratt* was viewed after the fashion of James Thornhill (compare Thornhill's *Selfportrait* in the National Portrait Gallery, Fig. 59). Seen at an angle, the chest slants back, which makes the torso look slim. The head is thrust energetically around to face the beholder from across the shoulder. The bright mass of the hair and face is divided into two slender halves—the central parting of the wig is cleverly utilized toward that end. The expression of elasticity to which all these devices contributed was further enhanced by the spacing. With much unoccupied space around, the head reminds one of a slender boat's prow forging through the water.

A change is also noticeable in Smibert's technique. The open brushwork of his early likenesses was completely lost under the smooth and even spread of his later paint. The flesh of the *Reverend James MacSparren* (Fig. 75) was modelled by means of disjointed spots, green for the shadows and pink for the lights; at close range the construction suggests the timid efforts of some would-be impressionist. In other early portraits, like the *Joseph Crawford* (Hartford, Conn., Athenæum), even the monotonous gray of a wig was rendered more cheerful by a few little specks of pink.

What probably accounted for Smibert's efforts, during the first ten years in Boston, to meet the taste of colonial clients at least halfway was the fact that his European training placed his work technically far above that of his provincial forerunners and contemporaries. When the colonial worthies objected to them, the painter toned down his metropolitan mannerisms. The toning down is evident when some of his portraits are compared with the English portraits that inspired them. Fashionable British attitudes were preserved, but they were stripped of pomposity. What made his portraits look less urbane than the English from which they derived was often only a more ponderous outline, a more massive design of the wig, a simplification in the forms of the scarf or a less supercilious carriage of the body.

The British influence Smibert brought to America is most clearly set forth in certain classes of paintings that were unfamiliar in New England, but extremely fashionable in the London of the 'thirties; to wit, "conversation pieces" and full-length portraits.

His first painting in the New World, *Dean Berkeley and his Entourage* (signed and dated 1729, Yale University Museum, Fig. 3), was a conversation piece with eight figures: Dean Berkeley is the commanding figure on the right; Smibert himself stands opposite on the left; the central group includes Mrs. Berkeley and her child, Mr. Moffat, Miss Hancock and the Secretary to the Dean. Until 1729, portraits of more than one person at a time were unknown in America.

The "conversation piece" had a long history in England. An uninterrupted line leads from Hans Holbein's *Family of Sir Thomas More,* of 1527, to the conversation pieces of Hogarth and Gainsborough. Smibert, it should be remembered, left England before Hogarth gave the old tradition its fresh bloom. Yet Smibert was experienced in the particular problems of the group portrait. On a short visit to Scotland after his return from Florence in 1720, he had painted *The Family of Lord Cullen.* Four years later, in London, he painted his companions of the "Rose and Crown" club, including his friends, painters Wooton and Gibson, and sculptor Bird.[21] And still later, in America, Smibert tried his hand more than once on conversation pieces.[22] *Mr. and Mrs. Johannes Schuyler*

[21]William T. Whitley, *op. cit.,* pp. 67 f., mentions that a sketch of the composition is preserved in Bird's notebooks.

[22]The *Berkeley* group was no doubt one of the two "conversation pieces" valued at a total of £23/6/8 in the inventory of Smibert's estate that was witnessed, among others, by John Greenwood, on Sept. 22, 1752. The other may have been that "unfinished picture of the ancient philosophers" mentioned by Chas. W. Peale after a visit to Smibert's studio in 1768. "Some groups of figures" which he also noted may or may not have been Smibert's own work.

(New York, Historical Society), the only group that still exists besides the Berkeley picture, has been very unfortunately cut down and patched together; the original composition can be at best surmised.[23]

*Dean Berkeley's Entourage* was a picture without precedent in the colonies. Its warm coloration and its solid design were altogether new. Nobody on this side of the Atlantic, except on a visit to England or the European continent, had seen such a large composition and such striking details. There was nothing in America to match the energetic design of the Dean's right hand gripping a book. An English connoisseur, more familiar with Hamilton's or Hogarth's informal conversation pieces, would have found the large figures somewhat old-fashioned, their postures too studied, and the pillared hall with the view on Narragansett Bay no longer *en vogue*. But residents of Rhode Island and Boston (whither the painting was removed when the Dean went home) must have found the whole thing extremely modern.[24]

Full-length portraits were no less of a novelty in colonial New England than were conversation pieces. Smibert's earliest full-lengths, *Mr. and Mrs. William Brown of Brownhall* (Johns Hopkins University, Figs. 60, 61), were painted at the end of the

[23]I have no doubt that the attribution to Smibert by William Savitzky is correct (*The New York Historical Society Quarterly Bulletin,* Vol. XVIII, July, 1934, pp. 19 ff.). Face, dress, and the "Michael Dahl posture" of Mr. Schuyler are in Smibert's manner of *circa* 1730 (*cf.* his *Lt. Gov. Wm. Tailer,* in the collection of Mrs. Luke V. Lockwood, Stamford, Conn.).

[24]In preparation for his first great canvas, Smibert painted a single likeness of *Mrs. Berkeley* (not extant) and at least two single likenesses of *George Berkeley,* the one which has been mentioned (London, National Portrait Gallery) and another one of 1728, in the Worcester Art Museum. In point of style, the portrait of *Mrs. Francis Brinley and Her Little Son* (1729, once owned by Mrs. H. Wharton) is closely related to the group of Mrs. Berkeley and her child in the *Berkeley Entourage*. That makes me doubt Henry W. Foote's suggestion (*New England Quarterly,* VIII, p. 27) that the child on Mrs. Berkeley's lap was painted in later; it may, of course, have been retouched in 1731, when the Dean stopped over at Boston on his way back to Ireland.

'thirties or in the early 'forties,[25] that is, at a time when the artist was beginning to relinquish the plainspoken colonialism of his earlier portraits of Americans for a more *de rigueur* British manner of representation.

In England, full-length portraits were always considered the most representative class of likeness, a class reserved almost exclusively for grandees. In New England, where modesty was deemed a supreme virtue, and in the democratic atmosphere of New York, busts or small-scale three-quarter lengths had so far been alone admitted. The portraits of *Mr. and Mrs. Brown* were of unusually large size—eight by four feet on the average. This as well as the fact that they were the first of their kind in the colonies[26]—a fact of which commissioners and artist must have been fully aware—should preclude any doubts as to the authenticity of one of the two paintings.[27]

The ostentatious attitudes of both figures are distinctly reminiscent of Kneller. *Mrs. Brown's,* in particular, reminds one of the

[25]The earliest possible date is 1737, the year of the marriage of William Brown and Mary Burnett. The latest possible date is 1745, the year of the wife's death.

[26]One of the earliest full-lengths now in the United States, *Elihu Yale* (dated 1717, Yale Museum of Fine Arts), was painted in England by Enoch Zeeman in his twenty-third year. Note, however, that full-length views were the rule in America since early colonial days if the subjects were infants, such as the *Gibbs Children* of 1670 (Fig. 28). A very curious example of about 1712, painted by Justus E. Kühn, is owned by the Maryland Historical Society: the small but pompous likeness of little *Eleanor Darnall* posed with her dog on an ornate terrace overlooking a park and an architectural background.

[27]Alan Burroughs would ascribe the portrait of *Mrs. Brown* to an unknown, less gifted, assistant of Smibert. Sometimes, be it admitted, reasons like mine advanced above against Mr. Burroughs' query are not in point. I have myself doubted the authenticity of the *Sir William Pepperell* (1745–47, Essex Institute, Salem, Mass.), a picture which is far better documented than the full-length of *Mrs. Brown;* namely, by Peter Pelham's engraving of 1747, which, while it is not a full-length but a three-quarter length, states by the legend that the original painting was Smibert's. Were it not for the legend on Pelham's engraving, I should never believe that Smibert had anything to do with the

"Hampton Court Beauties."[28] Less grandiloquent is the full-length of *Sir Peter Warren* (Portsmouth, N. H., Athenæum), which was painted in 1746; the date is inscribed on the portrait of *Lady (de Lancey) Warren* (Thomas B. Clarke collection). Here the contour is free of ornamental frills and the lighting is quieter and more solid.

Smibert was an alienator from the archaic colonial tradition rather than an advocate of it. If his paintings are viewed alone, this is less apparent than if his art is projected as a whole against the background of what American painting was at the time of his arrival and what it was at the time of his death, when his influence had taken effect. Other British artists came with their mannerisms on brief visits to New England; we shall hear more of one of them. But Smibert's influence was permanent.

Moreover, painting was only one of his several "agencies." Other equally effective transmitters of European taste were his art collections and his art store, where he sold "the best mezzotints, Italian, French, Dutch, and English prints, in frames and glasses, or without."[29] Another "picture store" was run by William Price,[30] but only Smibert carried the things a practising artist wanted, all the way from silver and gold leaf, fan mounts, canvases, palette knives, brushes and pigments, to books on perspective and European works of art. Among these the "landskips" were of great consequence for

---

monstrous painting in which the obese, red-coated victor of Louisburg appears to have been pasted upon a landscape-backdrop. The complete lack of atmosphere and modelling shadows (for instance, on the board-like red coat) ranks the picture with signboards rather than with known portraits by Smibert. The execrable hands alone suggest that, if Smibert's name must be attached, it can be only in a very general way. The execution is by some very inferior assistant. At least this is my opinion after having seen the picture several times in its rather dark and remote place in the Essex Institute.

[28]Compare Kneller's *Lady Middleton,* masked as a shepherdess with crook and lamb (Fig. 62).

[29]Advertisements in *Boston News Letter* and *Boston Gazette,* October, 1743.

[30]Carl Bridenbaugh, *op. cit.,* p. 454 f.

the future of art in America. Smibert had an additional forty-three of them in his private collection.

The late start of landscape painting in America is not surprising. It is a common fallacy that the art of landscaping springs from admiration of the scenery in which one lives. England was just as slow to accept landscape painting as America, and the Italian "picturesque" type which at first was the only popular type in England had nothing to do with the British scenery. Richard Wilson, "the father of English landscape painting," did not paint his views of Wales until very late in life. But even his early compositions in the manner of Poussin, Claude, or Canaletto, were criticized by Sir Joshua Reynolds for not transcending "common nature." It took all the time until the early nineteenth century before Old Crome painted the Slate Quarries of Ambleside, Constable the sun-lashed skies of Surrey, and Turner the Great Western Railway steaming through a sweeping rain.

America had to wait quite as long; partly because American painters were inexperienced, partly because the outlook of the American public was more materialistic. Less than the English could they see any value in picturesque scenery, except perhaps on wallpaper. Scraps of landscape descriptions in early colonial diaries plainly show that nature's beauty was associated with nature's utility. "Yea, in May you shall see the woods and fields so curiously bedecked with roses and an innumerable multitude of delightful flowers . . . that you may behold nature contending with art, and striving to equal if not excel many gardens in England," wrote Daniel Denton in 1679 of Long Island, "nay, did we know the virtue of all these plants and herbs growing there (which time may more discover) many are of the opinion, and the natives do affirm, that there is no disease common to the country, but may be cured without materials from other nations."[31] In the early period of indus-

[31] *Brief Description of Long Island,* quoted here from *American Memory,* assembled and edited by Henri Beston, New York (Farrar and Rinehart, Inc.), 1937, p. 31.

trialization the materialism of the American public may have been even more pronounced than in the early period of agricultural conquest. Here is a comment of a British observer in the America of 1834: "Scenery meant nothing. . . . To the American a waterfall is a motive power for his machinery, a mill privilege; an old building is a quarry for bricks and stones, which he works without the least remorse."[32]

When "things in the landskip way" came into demand in the New England of the seventeen-hundred-and-thirties and 'forties, landscape prints imported from England proved extremely helpful. They stimulated an artist's imagination. They showed him how to select motives and how to arrange them in a picture. Smibert ordered two different kinds from his agent in London: imaginative picturesque compositions, such as the *Antiquities* of Panini, which were mentioned earlier in this chapter; and topographical landscapes, such as *Views from Greenwich*. The former, being more for the enjoyment of the mind than the eye, tempted Smibert to "divert himself" with that particular genre in his late years, when his eyesight was growing dim. His early landscape paintings have perished; William Williams possessed a few of them and showed them to Benjamin West. But from the backgrounds of his portraits it is evident that he consulted foreign prints. To be ready in an emergency, he ordered from London "a set of ships published by Lemprière for to be used in a distant view of portraits of merchants, who chuse such."

The topographical landscapes shipped from London may have encouraged Smibert's young friend, Nathaniel Emmons (1704–40), to try himself, for the first time in America, on *River banks and rural scenes*. These were probably not any more "realistic" than Richard Wilson's English river scenes (which were painted a few decades later). Still, they so impressed a contemporary writer that he declared Emmons was "the greatest master ever born in this

[32]Quotation after James T. Adams, *The Epic of America* (Boston), 1934, p. 189.

country." Unfortunately, Emmons died at thirty-six and no certain work of his has survived either to prove or disprove the validity of such high opinion.

But what little we know from hearsay implies that Smibert's art store and studio were centers of the British influence. John Smibert's residence, marked by the master's ornamental sign and containing his collection "in the painter's room upstairs, an appropriate appartment lined with green cloth or baise," was preserved like a shrine. Before 1740, when Smibert took it over, it had been the home of Nathaniel Emmons. After 1751, Smibert's pupils, John Furnass and Samuel Minot, moved in. Charles Wilson Peale visited there in 1768. A frequent caller was John Copley, who lived only a short distance away. Eventually, John Trumbull rented the place as did, still later, John Johnston and Washington Allston. In everything but in name, Smibert's house was the first British academy in New England.

Smibert, I repeat, was not alone responsible for spreading the British tradition in America. Certain other lesser painters of Great Britain honored the colonies with brief calls. By this time, they even visited the South.

During the archaic period art had no place in the South.[33] Local

[33]On this point I must contradict the statement of Philip Alexander Bruce (*Economic History of Virginia in the Seventeenth Century,* New York, 1907, II, p. 174): "Paintings . . . were not entirely absent from the homes of the most prosperous planters." Mr. Bruce offers excerpts from inventories of estates in evidence. With one exception, however,—a portrait of an English Judge in the house of Colonel Thos. Ludlow—the twenty *pictures* cited by Mr. Bruce were doubtless cheap prints (valued at one shilling a piece!). In each of the four households mentioned, the pictures came in sets of five and their low valuation makes it further unlikely that they were paintings. Smibert's papers seem to me to corroborate my theory. In Smibert's estate of 1752 there is mention of 13 *landskips* and 41 *history pieces* besides single likenesses and *conversation pieces.* The appraisal shows that landskips and history pieces were prints (partly, as we have seen, by Panini, partly by English engravers). As against 2 conversation pieces valued at £23/6/8, the entire batch of 54 landskips and history pieces was valued at only £18/13/0; that is, at £4/13/8 less than two portrait groups.

conditions there were unfavorable to its growth. In the North there were towns where a limner could settle and gain some reputation before he went on the road. In the South there were only widely scattered plantations.

In 1736, or thereabouts, Charles Bridges came from London to paint the aristocrats of Virginia in the approved society style of London—no doubt to the satisfaction of the illustrious Spotswood and Byrd families, whose scions eventually preferred having their likenesses painted by Sir Joshua Reynolds. Colonel William Byrd of Westover was fully aware, however, that Mr. Bridges was not quite first-rate. Introducing the newcomer by letter to his neighbors as a potential "sergeant painter of Virginia," he added, "he has not the hand of Lily or Kneller." Bridges knew all the conventional tricks, particularly those of Michael Dahl. His portraits were veritable object lessons of Hogarth's theory that "phiz mongers, if they have silks and satins and velvets to dress their laymen, can carry on a very profitable manufactory without a ray of genius."

Speaking of Bridges' portraits, Virgil Barker says, "they are as essential to a comprehension of the sort of society which existed in the South as is the narrative of Bacon's Rebellion."[34] For that reason I think it revealing to see Bridges side by side with Smibert. Both were spokesmen of the British tradition, but they worked in different colonial regions. The New England sobriety in Smibert's likenesses may be the reason why critics have mistaken him for a typical representative of the American tradition. This would have been impossible to say of the "silks and satins and velvets" of such painters as Bridges; Smibert was to a much greater degree an American painter. Still, both he and Bridges were trained in Europe. To see the contrast we shall now proceed to Robert Feke.

[34] *An Introduction to American Painting, op. cit.*, p. 7.

## CHAPTER THREE

# ROBERT FEKE

### I. *Feke in New York*

ROBERT FEKE (1705–*circa* 1752) has been given late recognition. In 1834 William Dunlap gave him a sentence of twenty-five words (as against a dozen pages on Smibert).[1] In 1904 Samuel Isham believed half a sentence of fifteen words to be enough.[2] Then the tide turned. A learned paper on Feke was published in 1907,[3] and the first comprehensive book in 1930.[4] But the time for a general comprehension of the artist's importance seems still to be far away. I have mentioned the fact that Alan Burroughs makes of Feke a mere campfollower of the British school. As late as 1938, Christian Brinton refers to "the accomplished mannerist that was Feke."[5]

The dearth of information on his life is the chief reason for this neglect and misunderstanding of Robert Feke. Some historians of art will expatiate on an artist's life if it is documented and will illustrate their discourse with his pictures if they are available; if they are not, it does not really matter. Unfortunately, the history of Feke rests almost exclusively on his paintings. His life

[1]Dunlap's *History, op. cit.,* I, p. 17.

[2]Samuel Isham, *American Painting* (1904), New Edition with supplemental chapters by Royal Cortissoz, New York (The Macmillan Company), 1936, p. 17.

[3]William C. Poland, *Robert Feke, the Early Newport Portrait Painter* (Providence, Rhode Island Historical Society), 1907.

[4]Henry Wilder Foote, *Robert Feke, Colonial Portrait Painter,* Cambridge, Mass. (Harvard University Press), 1930.

[5]Gustavus Hesselius, *op. cit.,* p. 17.

story is obscure. First-hand sources are missing. The name of Robert Feke was not mentioned in either news sheets or letters of his time and appears but twice in diaries. There are a few meager entries in church records pertaining to him and members of his family. Fragments of an oral family tradition have been published sporadically since 1859.[6] As was inevitable in the course of over a hundred years, the tradition was jumbled and embroidered as grandfathers told fathers and fathers told sons the rumors about an ancestor of early colonial times who had been a black sheep—not a minister like themselves, but an artist—and that he had been through strange adventures.

The Feke family was of old Norfolk stock. Robert's great-grandfather came to Massachusetts with Governor Winthrop in 1630. The earliest manifestation of Robert's artistic talent is his *Self-portrait* (Belmont, Mass., Henry W. Foote, Fig. 63). It was painted about 1725 or, at the very latest, 1730.[7] Some time before, Robert was ejected from his paternal home at Oyster Bay, Long Island, by his father, a Baptist preacher, who "went so far in his resentment as to follow him to the water and there forbid him to enter it on pain of disinheritance."

Finding that the reason for this ejection cannot have been resentment over matters of faith, as the family tradition has it, Mr. Foote would dismiss the whole source. But his suggestion that it was not

[6]In *Dawson's Magazine*, 1859, 1860, 1878. Reprints *in extenso* are appended to H. W. Foote's biography of Robert Feke.

[7]Alan Burroughs (*loc. cit.*, p. 43) would move it to within five or six years of 1741 on the ground that the subject was older than twenty, perhaps as old as thirty-five. He says that Isaac Royall, represented at the age of twenty-two in the *Isaac Royall Family Picture* (Fig. 4), looks younger than Feke. This argument may be parried with the portrait of *Mrs. Feke* (Providence, R. I.), who certainly looks considerably older than thirty-two (born in 1718; Feke's artistic production terminated in 1750). Besides, Royall was an unusually suave-looking man of very regular features. The painter, however, had a most characteristic face: "long and pale, with a sharp nose, large, searching eyes and long, black and curly hair" (according to Doctor Hamilton's description). Such people are apt to look older than their age.

Robert "the painter" at all who was thrown out of the house sidetracks the issue. Why dismiss a valuable source *in toto* if its content is found to be inconsistent with other known facts in only one point? In such an oral tradition, concerned with only one person, an error in regard to that person is less likely to occur than is an error in regard to why something happened to that person. In a family of ministers, matters of faith usually take precedence over other matters with which they are less familiar, for instance the affairs of an artist. What seems to have happened in this case is this: In the course of a century the fact that the son was ejected was still remembered, but not what had been the cause of the father's wrath. Religious disagreement was thought most likely. I think a better reason may be found without sacrificing the historical source; namely, the Baptist preacher ejected his son when he discovered that he was going in for art.

The *Selfportrait* proves that Feke was no novice in that field. Furthermore, it reveals to what influence he was exposed at the time. It has nothing of the fetching grace of Kneller and the British school. What was floating before the young artist's mind when he painted his grave face and the eloquent eyes was colonial character portraits. The composition, showing the face from in front, the body in profile, and no hands at all, is rather flat and wooden. Angles and rigid lines are used where painters of British training would have preferred flowing curves.

A half-length likeness of Feke's little niece, *Levinah ("Phiany") Cook* (1732, Media, Pa., Robert Feeks Cox), must have been painted shortly before he went to New York, for on the back of the canvas the address where it was to be shipped is given: "To Robert Feke, at Mr. Judea Hayes in New York." Except for the searching gaze of the child's large eyes, which is a characteristic trait of Feke's style, the provincial picture of the little girl might have been done by any of the early New York limners. It is quite free of those British mannerisms which Smibert, at that very time, applied to his likenesses of children, such as the fidgety and ostentatious infant on the lap of *Mrs. Francis Brinley,* or the child in the painting of *Dean Berkeley's Entourage.*

During the nine following years, from 1732 to 1741, the young painter was not in America. And with no paintings of his for that period extant, and no mention of his name anywhere in the colonies, the tradition that "he was voyaging abroad" suggests quite naturally that he crossed the ocean for travels in Italy; suggests that he was doing what every young English artist of the eighteenth century deemed important. In his fourteenth "Discourse," Sir Joshua identified the continental tour with "academic education." An added casual note that during his absence from home Feke "was made a prisoner and carried into Spain" confirms my suspicion. For if a foreigner happened to be travelling in the region of Naples or Sicily in 1733 and was not cautious he was almost certain to get into trouble with the Spaniards. It was the time of the Polish War of Succession. Spain was defending the cause of Stanislaus Lescinski against Austria and Russia. She was fighting on the side of Sardinia and France, and the theatre of war was South Italy. If any one was careless enough to cross to the islands on an enemy boat, he took a chance of being made a prize by Spanish mariners and of being carried off to Spain.

My interpretation of the source sounds reasonable enough. Students of other books on Feke will observe that it differs from the way it has been read by William C. Poland and Henry Wilder Foote. Indeed, the difference is such that a minimum of defense on my part is indispensable. I shall limit my discussion to two counts.

## II. *Feke, the Mariner*

In the marriage certificates of Robert Feke's two daughters, drawn up after their father's death, on October 15, 1767, his profession is given as *mariner deceased.* This document has caused a good deal of confusion. Lawrence Park, H. W. Foote, Alan Burroughs, *et al.,* take it for granted that Feke was a seaman since his early years and buttress this with a passage from the "family tradition" saying that "as a young man he was several years absent on voyages abroad." I raise the question whether it is permissible to link these two unrelated sources of reference. The marriage certificate conveys only one thing with certainty and that is that Robert Feke was no longer a face-painter but a mariner at the time of his death. Whether or not he was a mariner in earlier days remains to be seen from other sources.

That "he left his home and voyaged abroad" does not imply that he was a sailor; in fact, that implication would be ludicrous without the other document. Feke was an Englishman born in the colonies and an artist. As I already have said, for any English-born artist who could afford it, it was a standard part of his education to make a continental tour. Smibert made the tour; eventually Benjamin West and Copley made it too. Why should Feke not have made it? It is all very well to point out the maritime atmosphere of Newport, its excellent harbor, its shipyards and overseas trade. Feke did not come to Newport until the 'forties. But quite apart from that, did not Copley and West come from the equally famous ports of Boston and Philadelphia? Has that fact induced any one to interpret their "leaving home and voyaging abroad" as their becoming *mariners*? Certainly not.

Is there any other evidence of Feke having been a mariner in his early years? The answer is, No. All descriptions of an earlier day refer to him as an artist and an artist alone. The word-picture of him, drawn in Doctor Hamilton's *Itinerarium,* mentions "a painter, the most extraordinary genius I ever knew," and, as Henry W. Foote must admit, "certainly does not read like the description of a seafaring man." Nor does Feke's latest *Selfportrait* (Fig. 64) look like one. It shows him sitting, brush in hand, before the easel. Doctor Hamilton, whose ears were open to gossip, would have been the last person on earth to omit the queer blend of sailor and painter if he had heard it mentioned in Newport.

In trying to solve the mystery of the document of 1767, Henry

W. Foote asks, 'Why was it that this man, who for nearly a decade before his death, and probably longer, was a professional portrait painter in Newport, and whose work was in demand in Boston and Philadelphia, was still remembered as a 'mariner'?" The answer is made difficult only by the word "still" in Mr. Foote's question. He was remembered as a mariner because he had changed to that profession before he disappeared from Newport and died abroad.

The change to another profession at the age of forty-four was not as erratic as it may seem to any one who is not familiar with conditions at Newport in the 'fifties. Still, if it should have been erratic, let it be remembered that unsteadiness was in the blood of the Fekes. Of this Mr. Foote gives a lively picture: the great-grandfather "unsettled and troubled in his understanding and brain"; John, who deserted Puritanism for the Quaker's faith; Robert "the preacher," who quit the Quakers and joined the Baptists; the painter himself, who was constantly on the move; his youngest son, Charles, the apothecary, who was considered an eccentric by some of his fellow citizens.

That Feke actually did go to sea in his forty-fourth year seems to me evident from the tradition that he sailed to Barbados (rather than Bermuda) after 1750, and, as Mr. Foote suggests, may have made several crossings before he died on that island, perhaps in November of 1752. He certainly had good reason to change to seafaring. In order to support his steadily increasing family he needed considerably more than the meager income forthcoming from a few likenesses of the residents of Newport and the vicinity. It may be well to remember that, when it was a question of how to make "real money," the particular business set-up of Newport offered much more profitable jobs. All one had to do was to get in, no matter in what capacity, on the Newport specialty known as *the triangular trade:* Molasses imported from Barbados; made into rum at Newport; exchanged for Negroes in Africa; Negroes exchanged in Barbados for more molasses; more molasses made into more rum in Newport; more rum exchanged for more Negroes in

Africa; and so on, *ad infinitum*. Everybody was growing rich in this triangular trade, and there were many possible ways of sharing the profits. That is probably why Robert Feke became a skipper when he got into financial straits. We are prone to size up the economic situation of the colonies by the standards derived from the period of the Revolution and forget that around 1750, by virtue of the machinery just described, the foreign trade of the small town of Newport was greater than that of New York.

Incidentally, Robert Feke was not the last of the family to go to sea. His eldest son eventually went down with an English trading vessel in the English Channel.

## III. *Feke's Imprisonment in Spain*

Another puzzle to Robert Feke's biographers has been his imprisonment in Spain. It has been connected quite unnecessarily with his seafaring. The source for it is the same from which the confusion about the *mariner* came: "He then left the house of his youth, and was several years absent on voyages abroad, in one of which he was taken prisoner and carried into Spain, where, in the solitude of his prison, he succeeded in procuring paints and brushes, and employed himself of means of returning to his own country. He soon thereafter settled and married in Newport, cultivated his talents and painted portraits."[8]

Were it not for the *idée fixe* that all this must have happened to a *mariner,* of which, in this connection, there is no mention whatsoever, the story would never have been so incredibly misread. To an unbiased reader it simply gives information about the adventures of an artist who went to Europe for study, got into some scrape, was put in prison, extricated himself, and returned home. It is noteworthy that Feke, according to other records, did come home precisely at the time mentioned in this source, namely, "shortly before his marriage," which took place in Newport in 1742. His first

[8]*Dawson's Historical Magazine* (1860), Vol. IV, p. 20.

dated picture after the long absence, the *Isaac Royall Family Portrait,* is of 1741.

It has been pointed out above that the occasion for Feke's imprisonment was the War of the Polish Succession (1733–35), which was waged, largely by Spain, at the very time when Feke vanished from the American scene and in the very region where art students preferred to linger on their Grand Tour, to wit, in Naples and Sicily. Smibert also had been there in his twenty-eighth year. I have further told how I believe it happened that Robert Feke was "carried into Spain." There was nothing extraordinary in his paying his way home from what remuneration he received for the portraits he painted in the Spanish prison. Gilbert Stuart eventually defrayed the cost of his transfer from the London sponging house to Dublin, and from there to the United States, in exactly the same way. It all sounds reasonable, provided that Feke was sufficiently trained to stand the competition of the early eighteenth-century Spanish and French painters. He would hardly have made enough to pay for his crossing, if his pictures, as our source says, were "rude."

Is not my explanation less far-fetched than the current one which has Feke fighting as a sailor in the navy against Spain—for which no plausible occasion can be found? But the possibility that Feke might have studied in Italy, as everybody else did, did not enter the heads of his biographers. First, because an education in Italy had always been believed a privilege reserved for John Smibert.[9] Second, because no continental tour is specifically mentioned in the sources. Although it is not specifically mentioned, it is unmistakably implied. The fact that neither the Italian nor the Spanish art left appreciable traces of influence on Feke's manner of painting is no evidence against my contention.

Feke may have been held in Spain for years. Preliminaries of peace were drawn up in 1735, but the ultimate treaty of Vienna

[9]Henry Wilder Foote, in *The New England Quarterly,* VIII (1935), p. 22, says: "It may be doubted if there was any one in Boston, or, as for that matter, elsewhere in the colonies, who had an acquaintance with Italy comparable to Smibert's."

which meant release of the prisoners of war was not signed until 1738. The fact that Feke paid his way home out of what he made of his paintings indicates a prolonged stay in Spain.

My conjecture is not contradicted by the remark of Doctor Hamilton that Feke "never had any teaching." This may have been literally true as regards regular instruction in another painter's studio, but, apparently, it was a fad among eighteenth-century *dilettanti* to boast of the unlearnedness of their respective protégés in order to make their genius shine the more brilliantly. Lord Lyndhurst, the son of John Singleton Copley, contended that his father "was entirely self-taught," which was quite untrue.

On the other hand, my conjecture of Feke's travels is corroborated by the way he was received on his return to America in 1741. On his first visit to Boston, in that year, he was at once asked to paint a large conversation piece for Isaac Royall, the wealthiest man in the colony. The painting was to include four adults and a child; to wit, Isaac Royall, his South American wife and their baby, Mr. Royall's sister, Penelope, and Mrs. Royall's sister, Mary Palmer. It was to be hung in the Royall Mansion at Medford, one of the most magnificent homes in Massachusetts, located on the site of John Winthrop's ten-hill farm. This was the biggest commission so far assigned to any painter in Boston and it was the first commission for a conversation piece since Smibert's *Berkeley Entourage.*

Why was this important order given to a painter whose name had not been heard of in the city? Why did it not go to Smibert who was entrenched in Boston almost as if he were the sergeant painter of the city's first families? Or, if Smibert was too busy, why was it not awarded to another resident painter? For the past fifteen years Peter Pelham had painted and engraved many a distinguished Bostonian; his likeness of *Cotton Mather,* of 1727, was the first mezzotint produced in America.

Surely, Feke would not have been so honored had he come to Boston as just another colonial limner. But if he came as a "foreigner," then he was just the person young Royall was looking for.

His mansion at Medford shows that he was going in for "modernism"; it was the first residence in Massachusetts where the Negro slaves had a separate building for themselves. Now that Mr. Royall was going to have his family portrait painted, he would naturally want it to be by an artist who was conversant with the latest European manners.

## IV. *Feke's Art in New England*

I have often wondered whether Isaac Royall was not in the end disappointed with what he got. For Robert Feke's *Family of Isaac Royall* (Harvard University, Fig. 4) was anything but modern in the European sense. Excepting for its brilliant coloration, it rather resembled the old-fashioned work of the Boston limners. Its effect was not nearly as "European" as that of the *Berkeley Entourage* (Fig. 3), with which Smibert had introduced himself as a connoisseur of the latest British vogue twelve years before. Feke did not make his models bow gracefully right and left or cast glances up and down. He did not employ Smibert's studied alternation of the full-face, profile, and three-quarter-face views. Nor did he in gathering his figures into a group use Smibert's compositional cadence—I mean, that swaying contour which, like a garland, fell from the top left to the center of the canvas and rose again to the right top. In Feke's group, a tangent drawn to the three heads of the ladies would be a horizontal line inflexible as the table top behind which they are seen as rigid perpendiculars and in primitive frontality. Smibert's composition was "picturesque"; its masses were grouped and distributed over the width of the canvas like irregular clusters of trees across the lawns of an English eighteenth-century park. In contradistinction, Feke's composition is artless; the three women remind one of a bleak wall from which Isaac Royall stands forth like the chimney at the small end of a colonial clapboard house. At all events, in point of style, the *Isaac Royall Family Portrait* was far removed as the poles from an English conversation piece of the seventeen-hundred-and-forties; but it was closely related to the archaic limners. In 1729, Smibert had painted a British conversation piece of European people and had hung it as the first example of its kind in an American home. In 1741, Feke painted the first American conversation piece. Its people were colonists of long residence and its style was in the American tradition.

I would not venture any guess as to whether Robert Feke made a conscious effort to revive the indigenous tradition. After his long absence from America he may just have picked up the thread where he had dropped it nine years before. Manifestly, he considered the *Royall Family* the cornerstone of his career in his native country to which he was returning. Now that his journeyman's years were over and his master's years were to begin, he chose for his first commission the largest available canvas, did a most ambitious job, and signed his work on the back with the date of its completion and his full name—a thing he never did either before or after: *Finisht September 15th, 1741, by Robert Feke.*

As a matter of fact, the painting bears all the earmarks of an "early" work. In comparison to the *Berkeley Entourage,* it cannot be called anything but primitive. As to liveliness, Feke's three ladies compare unfavorably with Smibert's more differentiated faces and postures, and their unspacious arrangement falls short of Smibert's plastic amplitude.

Certainly nobody but a prophet could have foretold from these four likenesses that Feke was soon to become the master of the early colonial character portrait. But what stood out as shallow and unanimated in his first significant painting, was superseded in the next nine years by a character penetration more and more deep and intense, and a physical representation more and more tangible and modelled.

But before we proceed to a closer inspection of that development we must first set aside the work of one year which forms a curious enclave in Feke's œuvre, namely, the portraits he painted in Boston during the year 1748 and the early part of 1749. Unfortunately, the general opinion on Feke as an artist has been unduly influenced by these pictures though they are quite untypical. They were painted under a violent, but short-lived, impression of the London school.[10]

Earlier than in 1748 Feke occasionally betrayed his familiarity with English art practices. The influence of Thomas Hudson has often been mentioned. Inasmuch as it has been traced in some of the work Feke did before his trip to England, of which we shall hear presently, the influence must have come by way of mezzotint reproductions. Hudson's influence did not amount to much. In one

[10]The portraits in question are *James* and *William Bowdoin* and their respective wives (Walker Art Gallery of Bowdoin College, Brunswick, Me.); three members of the *Apthorp* family; the eminent lawyer *Oxenbridge Thacher and His Wife;* Superior Judge *Stephen Sewall; Richard Saltonstall;* and half-lengths of *Mr. and Mrs. Gersholm Flagg.*

A number of other likenesses should, I think, be removed from H. W. Foote's list: The *Ralph Inmans,* husband and wife (Boston, William Amory and Mrs. Leonard Opdycke); *Mrs. Benjamin Lynde* (Boston, F. E. Mosely); the portrait of *Thomas Goldthwaight* (Boston, Doctor John T. Bowen) is utterly incompatible with the early colonial manner and should be left in Copley's œuvre, at least until it can be proved (which I doubt it can) that such a suave painting was possible anywhere in the colonies during the lifetime of Robert Feke. The singularly large life-sized full-length of *General Samuel Waldo,* who died in 1759, offers an intriguing puzzle. It was attributed to John Smibert in the collection of Mrs. Lucy Flucker Thatcher, who bequeathed it to the Walker Art Gallery of Bowdoin College in 1855. There it is attributed to Robert Feke, but neither attribution seems tenable. While the general arrangement, especially the pose with the left hand gracefully poised above the hip, was familiar to Feke, comparison of the design of that hand and its outstretched forefinger with the similarly poised left hand of *James Bowdoin* (hung on the same wall beside the *Waldo* portrait) may satisfy any critical student who is familiar with the Morelli method, that the two hands cannot have been drawn by one and the same individual. Smibert, on the other hand, as evidenced by his full-lengths, cannot have been the splendid colorist who painted *General Waldo's* scarlet vest and brown, gold-trimmed coat. Nor was Smibert enough of a plastic designer to be credited with the forceful, almost virtuose, spacing of the figure in the landscape. It was rather Feke who had a knack for that. However, the plasticity of the stupendous head with its eloquent black eyes and masterful modelling so far outdistances anything known of Feke's that I have asked myself whether the head was not, perhaps, repainted by a younger and more advanced artist than either Smibert or Feke. Upon

case he may have inspired an entire posture.[11] In other instances, Hudson's "fashion plates" were consulted by Feke for ladies' dresses —particularly, their rotund metallic modelling—and, occasionally, for little mannerisms of conventionalization—*e.g.*, hard, crescent-shaped dabs of dark paint to indicate the impressions in a satin skirt, or serpentine flourishes of bright paint to indicate the high lights on a silken sleeve or bow.[12] Such mannerisms of flat dark or bright curlicues were common in English prints of the first half of the eighteenth century.

But in the year 1748 the English influence on Feke's art had a much more deep-reaching effect.

There is no evidence that the artist was in America in 1747 and I can now furnish evidence that he was in England in that year —which so far has been only suspected. My evidence is the portrait of *James Bowdoin,* wearing a coat of murrey-brown velvet (Fig. 70). In point of arrangement, posture, coloration and general mood, this portrait of Feke so nearly "imitates" the *Gentleman in a Murrey Velvet Coat,* painted by Joseph Highmore of London, in 1747 (London, National Gallery, Fig. 71), that Feke's acquaintance with that English picture must be inferred. He cannot

closer inspection the head—its emotive animation as well as its pictorial construction—appears to be out of keeping with the rest of the picture. As regards its forceful conception and execution, it reminds me of similar heads by Copley, for instance, the head in the full-length of *Colonel Jeremiah Lee,* of 1769, in the Boston Museum. In this context it may be remembered that General Waldo's daughter, Hannah, married Thomas Flucker whose portrait Copley painted in the early 'seventies; Mr. Flucker's portrait came to the Walker Gallery from the same bequest as the Waldo portrait.

[11]Compare Feke's "second" portrait of *Mrs. Tench Francis* (Bryn Mawr, Pa., Edward Shippen Willing, Fig. 65) with Hudson's *Mrs. Harvey* (Lympne Place, Fig. 66). The compositional type was current in Hudson's studio as early as 1747 and was eventually popularized in America by Joseph Blackburn; compare that painter's portrait of *Mrs. Margaret Cheseborough,* of 1754, in the Metropolitan Museum (Fig. 67).

[12]*Cf. Mrs. Tench Francis* (Fig. 65), *Mrs. John Channing seated* (William E. C. Eustis, Esq., Milton, Mass.), *"Miss McCall"* (Pennsylvania Academy), and the portrait of *Mrs. Wanton* in the Redwood Library at Newport.

have seen it anywhere but on Highmore's easel in 1747.[13] Feke's stay in London and his association there, probably with the kind of painters of whom Hogarth said, "the little praise due to their production ought, in most cases, to be given to the drapery man," caused Feke, for one year thereafter, to become a "fashion plate painter." In all four of the Bowdoin portraits, the stress is exclusively on niceties of attitude, gesture, and apparel. *William Bowdoin's* green coat, pink vest, and sky-blue handkerchief form an ensemble so conspicuously "good-looking" that I have caught myself forgetting to look at the man's face. I have seen other visitors to the Walker Gallery wax enthusiastic over *Mrs. William Bowdoin's* white satin dress and *Mrs. James Bowdoin's* ensemble of azure; but as personalities these images are so shallow that they fail to register at all. How little Feke, in that one year, was concerned with personal characteristics may be seen from the two Bowdoin wives. Judging by their vague family likeness, they might have been twins, though in fact they were not related at all.

This fashion-plate painting and similar British mannerisms have been unduly emphasized in the general appraisal of Robert Feke's art. Since these pictures of but one year which have bulked so large have now been disposed of for what they are worth, they need no longer obscure our comprehension of the true development of Feke throughout the other eight years of his activity in New England. This development was along entirely other lines. It was, I repeat, the development of an artist who set out in search of the human being.

[13]On p. 13 of this book I have pointed out that such portraits used to pass directly from the painter's studio into the model's home. Moreover, to watch an experienced master at work was the most popular method of study among colonial artists. Gilbert Stuart allowed young painters to watch him without charging a fee. Thomas Sully paid John Trumbull $100 for painting a portrait of Mrs. Sully and the privilege of watching the artist at work. Chester Harding paid a few dollars to limner Nelson for a portrait of Mrs. Harding, which he ordered only so he might learn how the limner did it; but limner Nelson put up a screen so that no one could see him at work.

After settling as a married man in Newport, in 1742, Robert Feke began to show his discernment of those subtle character traits which Smibert refused to honor in the faces of his sitters. And contrary to Smibert, who gradually deserted the straightforward colonial taste, Feke gravitated more and more toward a searching revelation of character. By 1745 he outshone Smibert as an analyzer of the human face. After that he advanced to rounded and modelled images of men and women which almost anticipated the early work of John Copley.

The first evidence of this development is a pair of likenesses of Newport Baptist divines, *The Reverend Thomas Hiscox* (Newport, R. I., Mrs. Cornelius Vanderbilt, Fig. 69), and *The Reverend John Callender* (Providence, R. I., Historical Society, Fig. 68), who united Robert Feke and Eleanor Cozzens in marriage. So remarkable is the difference in the expression of the two ministers that one is at first inclined to assume they were portrayed at different times. But such was not the case. Both portraits were jointly ordered in 1745 by Henry Collins of Newport and were jointly delivered by Robert Feke.

A less sensitive artist might have been tempted by the joint order to adopt a certain uniformity of expression for both likenesses. But not Feke. He painted two perfect opposites. Callender's face, drawn in gently rounded lines and modelled with a tender fusion of tranquil shadows, is the very image of a trustworthy friend; a man who had harmony within himself and could, therefore, restore harmony wherever there was discord among his fellow men. His is a beautiful head. Yet its beauty does not result from some preconceived formula of design which is adaptable to any kind of face. Characteristic anomalies in the physical formation of Callender's face are faithfully recorded; the left eye is larger than the right one and the mouth, with its left corner drawn down, is a little crooked.

But the *Reverend Hiscox*—what a contrast! Accommodating charm is completely absent from his tight-lipped, determined, self-righteous head. It seems carved from hickory wood with its angular lines, its keen oppositions of light and dark, its nose and eyebrows pointed within the foursquare face. His eyes look down on the beholder; they are not level with him, as are those of *John Callender*. As indicated by the foreshortened nostrils, Feke viewed the head from below; perhaps Hiscox was unusually tall.[14] Still, I cannot help feeling that by dint of his "underview" Feke wished to set forth self-approbation as a definite character trait of his model. The "humbleness" of this Christian was vouchsafed officially on his record; "he twice refused appointment as an 'Elder' and did not consent to serve as pastor until he was sixty-four."[15] But Feke, by the very position of Hiscox's head, revealed the reverse of that official humbleness. What Feke exposed was, literally, the Reverend's "toplofty" attitude toward any one whose record in heaven was less impeccable than his own.

One year later, in Philadelphia, Robert Feke painted *Williamina Moore* (Thomas B. Clarke collection, Fig. 72). If any one of the *Royall* ladies is compared with it, this portrait of 1746 evinces an even more striking advance in the direction of the character portrait.

This young woman of nineteen, groping with lovely tapering fingers of one hand for the petals of the roses she is holding in the other, is the most affable female portrait in all colonial painting, barring none, before 1746. But again it must be added that the affability is not conjured up by any one of the flattering contrivances fashionable in the British school. From the pretty Southern dolls, say, of Charles Bridges, or from the affected attitudinizing introduced at that time to the New England towns by other visiting "phiz mongers" from abroad, it was a far cry to Feke's psychological

[14]In 1624, Nicholas Hilliard, in his *Treatise on the Art of Limning* advised painters, ". . . if he [the sitter] be a very high person, lette him sitte a littel above, because generally men be under him, and will so Juge of the picture because they underview him." (*Cf.* Sir Richard R. Holmes, in *Burlington Magazine,* VIII, p. 315.)

[15]Henry W. Foote, *Robert Feke, op. cit.,* p. 156.

study. It is a character study based on the apparent conflict between the girl's want of outer comeliness and her abundance of inner *charme d'esprit.* The artist made no attempt to conceal the fact that Miss Moore was plain looking. He could have done so easily; a caressing illumination would have done the trick, or a pleasant play of curves. But nothing of the sort was done. Feke's design is fundamentally as terse and angular as that of any archaic limner. The nucleus of his composition is a nearly equilateral, diamond-shaped area formed by the arms which are sharply bent at the elbows. No English painter of 1746 would have approved of a pattern of construction so rectilinear, planimetric, and harshly pointed (but the archaic limner who portrayed *Elizabeth Paddy Wensley* would have approved of it heartily).

To the very end, a profound kinship to the primitive colonial painters is sensed in the paintings of Feke. It is that kinship which determines him as the constant in the growth of the American tradition in contrast to Smibert who was the deflective force. But what should be observed at the same time is Feke's progress. He respected the archaic limners, but he also guided colonial art out of archaic awkwardness and constraint. When he was painting the *Isaac Royall Picture,* he was still put out of countenance by the spatial relationship of the four figures at the table; in other words, the archaic plane-boundness still imposed an appreciable constraint upon him. But he broke away from it soon. Five years later, when he painted *Williamina Moore,* he was still timid where it came to making the figure recede into space. Nonetheless, thanks to his more developed clair-obscure, the girl's head, torso, dress, and hands were assuming a credible semblance of rotundity. Another four years and these restrictions were also overcome. In the opinion of the colonists, the voluminosity of the portrait of *Mrs. James Tilghman* (*circa* 1750, Madison, N. J., Mrs. Sidell Tilghman, Fig. 73) must have been stupendous. It was as if Feke had approached his canvas from the sculptor's point of view, using the painter's tools and media as if he were cutting the form from a block of stone.

I am not denying that the figure of *Mrs. Tilghman* still seems unfree, unable to move in the space she occupies. Feke was not destined to go the whole length of the development which he inaugurated. Yet when he vanished from America at the age of forty-four he had progressed a good ways; indeed, he had gone much farther in those nine years than most others. The ultimate emancipation from the fetters of archaism was the historic mission of John Copley. Thirteen years after Feke had painted *Mrs. James Tilghman,* Copley employed the same motif—a lady bearing a flower—for his portrait of *Mrs. Metcalf Bowler* (New York, Miss Alida Livingston, Fig. 74). Copley could represent nature unconstrained, liberated from archaic stiffness, but also—thanks to Robert Feke—liberated from British sophistication.

Viewed in the historic perspective of the eighteenth-century development, Robert Feke appears as the most important link between the archaic limners and John Copley. But let that not be understood to mean that Feke was but a link in a development. The fact that Copley progressed beyond him does not lessen the broad and deep significance of Feke's contributions. The very limitations of the primitive style enabled him to say things in his pictures that Copley could no longer say with the same forceful language.

For example, Feke could express himself through the medium of proportions that were normal in early colonial times, but outmoded in the middle colonial period of Copley.

Early colonial painters and architects were generally fond of squat proportions. In early likenesses the upper molding of the frame often weighed down on the crowns of men and women exactly as the low ceilings did on early colonial rooms, or the overhang of the roof pulled down over doors and windows, or the railing of the stairs lifted to the top joists with no clearing overhead. In every such instance, the effect is one of depression, no matter whether it was intentionally achieved or accidental. In the middle colonial period of Copley, and, increasingly, in the late colonial period of Gilbert Stuart, such oppressive proportions were supplanted by more soaring patterns that left breathing space above the persons. Even so, in rooms, stairwells, and façades of that period greater height was introduced and was rendered æsthetically effective by the use of slender windows, perpendicular wall trim, lofty pediments or clearings above the doors.

It is interesting that Robert Feke abided by the early colonial scheme of level proportions, while Smibert after a short while broke away from it, granting his models more and more elbow space and room above. Feke, however, narrowed the space of his later portraits more and more. *Williamina Moore* (Fig. 72) in the portrait of 1746, was not yet so cramped as was *Mrs. James Tilghman* (Fig. 73) in the portrait of about 1750. With his late likenesses, Feke seemingly returned to typically archaic proportions. It was no *return,* really, for there was a significant change. As Feke again packed his figures into very constrained spaces, he did not stress the proportion of breadth, as the archaic painters had done. Instead, he stressed the proportion of height. The late *Selfportrait* (*circa* 1750, Providence, R. I., the Misses Anna and Rhoda Bullock, Fig. 64) as well as *Mrs. Tilghman* evince the new proportion. They differ from all earlier portraits in that, despite the increase in voluminosity, the images no longer seem depressed, but uplifted —literally as well as metaphorically speaking. And that is very significant.

Feke's earlier likenesses were composed on the pattern of an expansive pyramid in which the head formed the apex. *Williamina Moore* is an example; other examples are *"Miss Mary McCall"* (Pennsylvania Academy) and *Mrs. Charles Willing* (1746, Rhinecliff, N. Y., Vincent Astor, Esquire). In the later portraits the heads surmount a substructure which is verticalized like a Greek herma —a very solemn form. I like to think that these unbending proportions sprang from a desire on the part of Robert Feke to deepen his characterization by endowing the individual likeness with the typical properties of Christian ethics. The personal features of *Mrs. Tilghman* are obvious to any one. One has to look deeper to find that they have been wedded to a pictorial symbol—that surging herma-pattern which betokens "the unstooping firmness of an upright soul." I would like to go even farther. To this ethical symbolism there was added a strong colonial note—the restricted space in which Feke's characters dwell in his late portraits. It is the treatment of space that makes the people he painted appear as "constrained" as they were in life. By means of the very pattern of his portraits Feke communicated this message of upright men and women surmounting day by day the narrow conditions of colonial life. Smibert said nothing of that. He made his persons parade on a spacious stage. That was British symbolism, befitting ladies and gentlemen of leisure.

I trust my readers will not misinterpret this analysis. I am far from suggesting any planful calculation on the part of Robert Feke, let alone an awareness of his artistic evolution. As most other painters, Feke probably reacted to instinct, rather than to plan or theory. But his instinct was a reflection of his personal temperament. And it is not the least thing that can be said in defense of the Americanism of Robert Feke's art, that his temperament was shaped by the blood of his American ancestors and the American milieu. How, then, did his temperament determine his style?

The artist's late *Selfportrait* (Fig. 64) reveals him as a person sedate and pedestrian. What little we know of his life shows that he was never in a hurry—he did not get properly started on his career until he was thirty-six and he delayed his marriage until he was thirty-seven. The tardy efflorescence of his art is another witness to his slow-moving temperament. If his brush strokes and his manner of drawing a line are examined graphologically, as ordinary "handwriting," they denote an apathetic disposition. His contour was ponderous. It moved *in tempo largo e maestoso*. The three-dimensionality of his forms resembles his contour in that it is compact and solid; his bent surfaces are broken up but slightly. With the exception of the portraits of 1748, none of his likenesses was delicately articulate and supple. His perception was as unsophisticated as a child's. His hand, despite its long and sensitive fingers, was heavy when it was modelling, even somewhat clumsy at times. His style was blunt rather than bland. But the bluntness of his expression should not be mistaken, as it so often has been, for incompetence. It was a vital and characteristic part of his portraits of colonists whose images passed through his temperament—a colonist's temperament. Feke was surely not aware of all that. In all likelihood he knew of no higher aim than to paint his sitters as faithfully from life as he could. But whether he knew it or not, he fostered the colonial tradition because the colonial spirit was in him.

## CHAPTER FOUR

# JOHN SINGLETON COPLEY IN NEW ENGLAND

### I. *Copley's Fame*

BENJAMIN WEST and John Singleton Copley were the first American painters who won public recognition in the Old World. They won recognition not for their Americanism, but for their adaptability; for their talent of making one forget that they were Americans. Copley, in particular, who came to London after twenty or more years of activity in New England, was an object lesson to his colleagues of the Royal Academy of what could become of a crude colonial face-painter if he conformed to the gentle standards of the British school. That was all his contemporaries could see.

We see it differently. We see the sad lot that befell colonial art when it was deserted by its greatest master. We may even feel bitter when we learn that Copley thereafter identified himself with the critical opinion of the Royal Academy of England in such a measure that he had nothing but ridicule for the painting of New England, which he himself had brought to its classic consummation. For colonial portraiture—that sturdy perennial which could not put forth growth anywhere except in the crude soil and the crisp air of the colonies—had been nursed by Copley alone after the older gardeners, Smibert and Feke, had finished their work. Benjamin West, born within a year of Copley, never really came to know that native flower. He disengaged himself early from his native country, went to Rome and London and there cultivated eclecticism —quite another plant, a hothouse product raised for the enjoyment of the fastidious connoisseurs of senescent Europe, but fundamentally worthless to the youthful people of the American seaboard.

In a measure commensurate with the growing fame of Benjamin

West, the colonial public lost faith in Copley's colonial work. After he had removed himself to London and was elected an R.A., they were no less convinced than he that what he painted in Europe was infinitely more significant than his colonial performance.

Shall we join in the recognition the eighteenth century gave to Copley's European success? Or shall we lament the decline of the colonial tradition that it entailed? It depends on what view the historian of art must take. Considering the development of American art from the English point of view, Copley's transfer to London was a blessing. The acquisition of British finesse improved his provincial technique. The addition to mere face-painting of allegorical and history painting, landscape, marine, and still-life was an expansion of the scope of colonial painting for which Americans had every reason to be thankful. Considering the development of American art from the American point of view, all these advantages were outweighed by the consequences that were inevitable when Copley not only surrendered the colonial tradition to British academic standards but ceded to West the leadership that by right should have been his.

The future of American art depended, as the future always does, on the accidental turns of its top men. It is futile to seek a definitive answer to the question, what would have become of colonial painting if Copley had stayed at home and had become the leading painter of the Revolution. It is futile because Copley did not stay. Nevertheless, it is pertinent to ask the question. To realize what Copley's desertion of America meant, we need only ponder the fact that today West's art is dead; that most of the paintings Copley did in London are forgotten; but that his colonial work lives. It is gaining in influence from year to year.

His contemporaries were in no position to realize that Copley was a constructive force in the development of colonial art. But for other reasons, his renown was great, in Boston as well as in London.

Charles Wilson Peale, an art student of twenty-seven, journeyed all the way from Annapolis to Boston to seek instruction from

Copley, who was thirty-one. Copley's personality so fascinated the fourteen-year-old John Trumbull that he decided on the career of a painter, in defiance of his governor-father's remonstrances. And so enduring was the first impression that Copley made on his young disciple that Trumbull's mature paintings bore the stamp of Copley's sober factualism though he never had a real lesson from him, and had studied under West. Copley magnetized laymen and artists alike. His authority was questioned by none. He changed the taste of the New England public until they no longer admired their primitive local painters. John Adams belittled the "miserable likenesses" that he remembered having seen in the Council Chamber of Town Hall, but praised Copley's likenesses for their "truth, nature and fact; you can scarcely help discoursing with them, asking questions and receiving answers."[1] What that praise amounted to may be gleaned from what the same writer, but a year later, admitted to the sculptor Binon: "I would not give sixpence for a picture of Raphael."[2]

Before long the very name "Copley" was to lend distinction to every family portrait to which it was attached and to cast glory on the family that owned one. "The possession of one of Copley's ancestral portraits is an American's best title to nobility."[3] It was quite consistent with his growing fame that Copley's name was ultimately even associated with George Washington. Having left the country in 1774, it was well-nigh impossible that Copley should have painted General Washington or President Washington. So he was said to have painted Washington, the Indian fighter. Fortunately, the miniature which was supposed to prove the point was found not to be Copley's work.

His name was known in London even before he got there. If his

[1]*Statesman and Friend,* Correspondence of John Adams with Benjamin Waterhouse, Boston, 1927. Letters of March 17 and April 15, 1817.

[2]William T. Whitley, *Gilbert Stuart* (Harvard University Press, Cambridge, Mass., 1932), p. 163.

[3]Frank W. Bayley, *The Life and Work of John S. Copley,* Boston (The Taylor Press), 1915, p. 18.

friend, Captain Bruce, may be trusted, no less a person than Sir Joshua Reynolds said that *The Boy with the Squirrel* "exceeded any portrait that Mr. West had ever done," and that, judging by its unusual merits, Copley, then twenty-eight years old, promised to become "one of the first painters of the world." No fair-minded critic in London questioned Reynolds' prophecy after Copley had successfully rid himself of his "provincial" manner. Indeed, the popularity of Copley's historic pictures soon began to alarm his colleagues in the Royal Academy. When he exhibited the *Death of the Earl of Chatham,* in 1781, and was bold enough to do so in a tent at Spring Gardens, instead of at Somerset House where the other Academicians held their exposition, the financial success unfavorably affected the revenues of the Academy; receipts of the season fell to nearly £1000 below those of the preceding year.[4] Ten years later the showing of *The Defeat of the Floating Batteries at Gibraltar* again reduced attendance at the official exhibition to "poor."[5] The "pavillion" in which Copley's canvas was exhibited (jealous colleagues called it a "booth") had to be dismantled several times and rebuilt elsewhere because the neighbors complained of the racket produced by the 60,000 visitors.

In view of what America owes to Copley's colonial painting it is interesting that he was a tory and never thought highly of the American people. The Birth of a Nation, he thought, was a dream removed by at least another century. According to an English fellow traveller on the way to Rome, Copley, in 1774, "solaced himself that if they go on in America for a hundred years to come, as they have for a hundred and fifty years past, they shall have an independent government . . . art would then be encouraged and great artists would arise." For the time being he foresaw only the worst. He scoffed at the intolerable narrow-mindedness of his fellow townsmen. In 1775, the American Revolution seemed to him an act of mob violence with most regrettable results: "Unhappy

[4]William T. Whitley, *Artists and Their Friends in England, op. cit.,* I, p. 357.
[5]William T. Whitley, *Ibid.,* II, p. 140.

and miserable people, once the happiest, now the most wretched."[6]

Circumstances forced him into this tory attitude. It so happened that the £15,000 worth of tea that was dumped into the harbor on the day of the Boston Tea Party belonged to Copley's father-in-law, Richard Clarke. Six months after Richard Clarke was run out of town, Copley shook the New England dust from his shoes. During his absence abroad certain smart speculators all but swindled him out of his eleven-acre farm on the east side of the Charles River. That is why Copley never returned.

## II. *Copley's Early Portraits*

John Singleton Copley was born on July 3, 1737. His Irish parents came to America about a year before his birth. Shortly thereafter his father, Richard, went to the West Indies and died there, leaving his widow to make a living in Boston as a tobacconist selling "the best Virginia tobacco, cut, pigtail and spun, of all sorts, by wholesale or retail, at the cheapest rates." The determination and perseverance of Mary Singleton Copley was inherited by her son John.

When Copley was eleven his mother married Peter Pelham, the friend of John Smibert. He had lived in Boston since 1726. In 1748 "the widow Copley formerly on the long Wharf" became "Mrs. Peter Pelham removed into Lindel's Row, against the Quaker Meeting House near the upper end of King's Street." Here she continued her tobacco business while her husband contributed to the maintenance of the family from what was forthcoming from his painting, mezzotinting and school for "reading, writing, needlework, dancing, and the art of painting on glass." Pelham soon discovered his stepson's precocious talent and gave the boy his first instruction in art. But when John was fourteen, Peter Pelham departed this life and Mary Pelham was once more faced with the responsibility of caring for the family. It was a little easier this time. The three sons of Pelham's first marriage were now of age.

[6]Letter to Mrs. Copley from Rome, July, 1775.

But in addition to John Copley there was a small child to provide for. This was Henry Pelham, John Copley's particular chum. The artist painted him, in 1765, as *The Boy with the Squirrel* (Fig. 90). He wrote to him whenever he was away from home; in New York, Philadelphia, Rome, or wherever he happened to be at the time. It was Henry whom he left in charge of his large estate on Beacon Hill when he went to Europe. Almost everything that is known about Copley's private life has been taken from the bulky correspondence between the painter and his stepbrother.[7]

The earliest extant work of Copley was done in Boston when he was sixteen. His last painting, *The Resurrection,* was done in London when he was seventy-six; that was three years before his death. The intervening sixty years divide into two large periods: twenty-one years in New England (1753–74), and forty years in London (1775–1815). The turning point was his European journey of fifteen months from the summer of 1774 to the autumn of 1775; seven of these were spent in Rome.

A long line of portraits of people from Massachusetts, Pennsylvania, and New York, painted in the first ten years of his career, show how Copley transformed the early colonial manner into the "classic" middle colonial. His work from 1765 to 1774 was the richest and most beautiful flower of the colonial painting of the eighteenth century. In saying this, I am viewing Copley's contribution to the history of American painting as a general evolutionary phenomenon, exactly as I would view Albrecht Dürer's transformation of the archaic manners of Martin Schongauer and Michael Wohlgemut, or Raphael's transformation of Perugino's timid expression into a style of grand simplicity, clarity, and plasticity. From the *Reverend William Welsteed* (Fig. 76), whom Copley painted at the age of sixteen, to the *Nathaniel Hurd* (Fig. 89), whom he painted when he was about twenty-seven, he ad-

[7] *The Letters and Papers of John Singleton Copley and Henry Pelham, 1739–1776.* Mass. Historical Society Proceedings, Vol. 71 (1914).

vanced consistently from rigidity to free movement, from relative flatness to three-dimensionality, from an observation of parts to a discernment of totality, from standard patterns to original compositions.

In the process of this evolution Copley ultimately found himself, realizing his uniqueness. From the more or less impersonal face-painter of the Boston School, that he was to begin with, he evolved into what we know as "John Copley."

The formative phase of Copley, from 1754 to 1764, was not different from the formative phase of any modern artist who happens to live in a town too provincial to afford the coveted measure of training. Copley could have depended on his eyes, which were uncommonly sensitive and which he enjoyed using. "There is a kind of luxury in seeing," he later declared, "as well as there is in eating and drinking; the more we indulge, the less are we to be restrained." (Again one is reminded of Albrecht Dürer who said *"des Menschen edelster Sinn ist das Gesicht."*) But in a relatively artless surrounding not even a budding genius can depend wholly on his observation. He must find out "how things are done." In groping for a method of painting Copley turned to whatever constructive criticism he could derive from the pictures that were in Boston.

The only real instruction he had was from his stepfather. Peter Pelham gave him a sound foundation. Its influence is sensed in the work of Copley almost until he left the colonies. It was no specific influence that could be traced in detail. It was the more basic influence of a training given by a professional engraver. Copley's entire colonial work bears the stamp of the engraver's approach, to wit, the steel-like precision of his drawing, his metallic modelling and his fundamental concern with "black-and-white" rather than with color. That was what Thomas Sully, the early Victorian painter of Philadelphia, had in mind when he criticized Copley's "hard terminations" and branded his coloration as "crude."[8] It was

[8]William Dunlap's *History, op. cit.*, I, p. 143.

not any more crude than Albrecht Dürer's coloration. It was something added. Most of Copley's colonial paintings could do without color and yet would not lose their graphic construction, force, and lucidity. To Copley, who was fundamentally a draughtsman, colors were not chromatic values so much as means by which to define plastic values. Colors did not interest him either as visual sensations or as elements of painterly construction. It is revealing that Copley's coloration was more sparkling when he was working with colored crayons than when he was using oils; for crayons are "graphic" media. He began at a very early time to employ pastels (as they are called today). His first portrait in that medium, *Richard Ward* (Rhode Island School of Design), was done in his seventeenth year.[9] Eight years later he wrote to Etienne Liotard to inquire where better crayons than those available in Boston could be had.

Nevertheless, Copley obtained fine effects of color harmony also in his oils, often by painting either in monochrome, as in the portrait of *Thomas Flucker* (1770–71, Bowdoin College), or nearly in monochrome, as in the *Benjamin Pickman* (Fig. 84) and the *Epes Sargent* (Fig. 86), where a warm gray is enlivened with little specks of scarlet and golden ocher. The most perfect example is the *Gov. Thomas Mifflin and His Wife* (1773, Historical Society of Pennsylvania), a harmony of two grays touched up with muffled spots of red, purple, and blue. In other instances Copley would intensify a single predominant color tone, as graphic artists do at times, by adding only touches of other colors; note the blue coat of *Daniel Henchman* (painted before 1761, Concord Art Association), and the blue dresses of *Mrs. Daniel Rogers* (1762, Miss Mary Rogers Roper) and *Mrs. Benjamin Pickman* (1763, Newport, R. I., The Misses Wetmore), the brown dresses, touched up with white and black, of *Mrs. Thomas Boylston* (1766, Fogg Art Museum of Har-

[9]Barbara Neville Parker and Anne Polling Wheeler, *John Singleton Copley,* Boston, Mass., 1938, p. 259, contend "this portrait cannot be definitely attributed [to Copley]." It is signed and dated 1754, and is in a perfect state of preservation. What more can be asked?

vard University, Fig. 5), and *Mrs. Sylvanus Bourne* (1766, Metropolitan Museum), and the burst of brownish pink in the *Nathaniel Hurd* (Cleveland Museum, Fig. 89). A desire to impress the metropolitan public of London accounts in all likelihood for the more ambitious attempts to widen the range of his palette after 1764. *The Boy with the Squirrel* (Fig. 90)—in blue, citron, rose and dark red—was intended for exhibition in London and "for an Exhibition," Copley wrote to Benjamin West, "something more may be expected, and the artist is greatly to be pitied, who cannot occasionally rise above the common level of his practise."[10] Although certain of his noble endeavors at that time brought the desired success, still his finest color schemes did not change the "draughtsmanlike" construction of his colonial portraits any more than a nice adaptation for orchestra changes an original composition for the piano.

In his quest for reliable guides who would aid a beginner's progress, Copley turned for advice to what prints or paintings were within reach—the work of Pelham, Smibert, and Feke. None of the three masters were there when Copley began to produce.

Feke left Boston in 1749 and two years later Peter Pelham and John Smibert died. So until the arrival of Joseph Blackburn, in the latter part of 1754, there was only the small fry left: John Johnston, the engraver, and the painters John Greenwood and Joseph Badger. The latter (1709–65), who is described chiefly as a glazier, house-painter, and sign-painter, was the best of the lot. But no inspiration came from his modest paintings which Copley could not have gotten more directly and boldly from the work of Feke and Smibert that was to be seen in the best Boston homes.[11]

[10]*Copley-Pelham Letters, loc. cit.,* Letter to West of Jan. 17, 1768.

[11]Judging by some of Badger's portraits of the period 1743–65 (as catalogued by the late Lawrence Park in *Mass. Historical Society Proceedings,* 1917), his manner was old-fashioned before he was old himself. The praise and admiration that Mr. Burroughs bestows on him would perhaps be merited if Badger's work fell in a less advanced period, which it doesn't. The portraits of *Mr. and Mrs. Orne* (Readville, Mass., Robt. Saltonstall), which even

Besides, the boy Copley must have known John Smibert personally quite as well as he knew Robert Feke, who spent more than a year in a house near Smibert's at the time when Mary Copley married Peter Pelham. At all events, it is certain that Copley sooner or later became acquainted with those paintings of Feke which hung in the houses of families that now patronized him as before they had patronized Robert Feke—the Royalls, the Apthorps, and the Bowdoins. Copley knew Smibert's work intimately, no doubt. Nevertheless, his early manner was more akin to Feke's. The *Mrs. William Whipple* (Milton, Mass., Alexander H. Ladd, Esquire), one of his very early portraits, looks like an unsuccessful attempt to duplicate Feke's *Mrs. James Bowdoin*. The attempt was more successful in the *Mrs. Joseph Mann* (1753, Melrose, Mass., Frederick H. Metcalf, Esquire). A more mature work, the *Edward Holyoke* of Harvard, seated in the President's chair (before 1760, Harvard University, Fig. 77), shows independent continuation of Feke's robust and stony plasticity. The "cubism" as well as the veracity of its design differs fundamentally from Smibert's manner.

As to these early works, however, one cannot always tell with certainty from where the decisive influences came. There were too many influences and sometimes they were not even American influences. In a later chapter I shall discuss a mythological subject piece of this period which drew its inspiration in all likelihood from French bookplates. In the portraits, even the Dutch trend of New York was mixed with the archaic and early colonial manner of New England.

---

Mr. Burroughs admits are "truly primitive," though dated 1757, are artistically far behind not only what young Copley had done three and four years earlier, but also behind the paintings of Smibert and Feke that were ten years earlier. Apparently Badger camped on the trail of others and never got beyond what had been stylish when he was in his thirties. Such an artisan may have instructed young Copley after Pelham's death in the elements of the limner's trade, but it is hyperbolic to say that "his bold and simple records of an unperplexed society foretold the best part of Copley's achievement." That would be a better description of Feke than it is of Badger.

The portrait of the *Reverend William Welsteed* (1753, Massachusetts Historical Society, Fig. 76), from which Copley made his first engraving at the age of sixteen,[12] was apparently patterned on something like Smibert's *Reverend MacSparren of 1729* (Bowdoin College, Fig. 75). The Welsteed portrait was more in the nature of a "caricature" than anything Smibert ever painted. Perhaps the *engraving* after Robert Feke's *Reverend Thomas Hiscox* gave Copley a lesson in characterization.

On the other hand, the difference between Feke's and Smibert's natural mastership and young Copley's dilettantish imitation is very noticeable. The *MacSparren* likeness is of a piece. There is no break in its visual unity. The *Welsteed* portrait, however, is not viewed as a whole. The head is isolated by one mode of seeing,

[12]According to tradition, the painting owned by the Massachusetts Historical Society is Copley's original oil after which he made the engraving. Recently Barbara Neville Parker and Anne Polling Wheeler (*loc. cit.*, p. 238) have maintained that the painting under question, while it looks to be contemporary, is not by Copley. "An X-ray shows that the brushstrokes are not Copley's . . . the authors' supposition is that Copley used the portrait as a model for his (lost) original and that he did the engraving from his own portrait." This construction is, I confess, a trifle too subtle for me to accept, on its strength alone, the refutation of the earliest known work of Copley. X-rays may reveal a good deal. They may, for example, reveal that the brushstrokes in a painting differ from the brushstrokes that were *predominant* in a painter's work in a particular period (but even that would not suffice to throw out any particular painting unless other and stronger evidence makes it advisable). But where the work of a boy of sixteen is under discussion, who like most beginners was probably given to technical experimentation, the difference of brushstrokes would not warrant precluding his painting even if there were many other paintings with different brushstrokes. But there is just one other painting of Copley's that bears the date 1753, and its companion piece which bears none may be taken for the other painting that is certainly of that year, the *Mr. and Mrs. Joseph Mann.* All other attributions to that year are arbitrary. I prefer to accept the likeness of the Massachusetts Historical Society as Copley's original painting. I cannot believe that young Copley painted the *Reverend Welsteed* from some other painter's original and yet had the audacity to say in the legend of his engraving that he *painted and engraved* the likeness. I accept it the more gladly since it bears all the earmarks of a beginner's work which one expects to find with young Copley, but not with some other more experienced painter.

the gown by another, and the flaps of the collar again by another. While Copley was quite successful in following Smibert's general pattern, he lost control of the whole and did not know how to proceed where the pattern gave out and left him dependent on his eye and hand alone, for instance when it came to the face. Smibert knew how to organize an entire portrait technically. *Reverend MacSparren's* head is no less mottled and modelled than is his clerical frock. The face of Reverend Welsteed, however, is weakly modelled, especially from the cheekbones down. As any drawing teacher knows from experience, it is there that a beginner finds the greatest difficulty in mastering the planes of the face plastically. Furthermore, young Copley's shadows were too little correlated really to "model" anything. Some of them were like flat ribbons and were poorly stressed—another typical sign of the beginner who renders objects more readily in linear terms than he does through the correct control of chiaroscuro values. The unmediated shadow which bounds the hair from the temple and the cheek on the right side of the face does not match the corresponding pale shadow on the left side of the face. And so on. In Smibert's portrait, due to a well-calculated balance of values of light and dark, the collar flaps do not stick out as an overstressed mass of white, as they do in Copley's painting because of a lack of corresponding values.

### III. *Copley and Joseph Blackburn*

In 1754, when Joseph Blackburn arrived from London with what must have seemed a wealth of foreign experience and inspiration, Copley began to exploit the ready-made picture patterns that the English painter probably sampled from his satchel. Blackburn descended, directly or indirectly, from Thomas Hudson's school. He was more familiar than Feke had been with the stock-in-trade of Hudson's portrait-shop, with its custom-made postures as well as its tricky manner of painting the texture of silk and rich materials.[13]

[13]As was pointed out in a footnote on p. 76, Blackburn's earliest dated portrait, *Mrs. Margaret Sylvester Cheseborough* of Newport (1754, Metropolitan

Blackburn was close to Copley from the time he set foot in Boston. Copley, then in his eighteenth year, perhaps saw in the visitor's manner of painting another, subtler variety of Robert Feke's manner.

Blackburn had, of course, certain advantages over the older artist. For one thing, he was a more discriminating colorist. The coloring of the likenesses of *Mr. and Mrs. James Otis* (Boston Museum) was something to marvel at in the Boston of 1755. Unprecedented was this luminous consonance of shiny white satin with light blue; this attunement of all chromatic values to the black of the hair and the gray of the eyes; ultimately, those opalescent flesh tints! Besides, Blackburn was conversant with new tricks that were becoming

---

Museum), was patterned on Hudson's *Mrs. Harvey,* a portrait probably "just out" when Blackburn sailed west, in 1752; and Robert Feke's *Mrs. Tench Francis,* it will be remembered, derived from some similar Hudson pose (*cf.* Figs. 65–67). Maybe, the kinship of these three paintings holds the clue to why Blackburn went to Boston and settled there until Copley's rising fame made it seem advisable for him to quit. It is curious that on his way from England Blackburn loitered at all the places where Feke had been popular before. This would even hold true of Blackburn's first halt in Bermuda, in 1753, if it could be proved that Feke died there, as one source says. It is true of Newport, where Mrs. Cheseborough resided (though family tradition says her portrait was painted in New York), and it is true of Boston where the journey terminated. It is all quite hypothetical, but this itinerary suggests at least the possibility that Blackburn had met Robert Feke in London and that, in 1752, when the news of Feke's death got abroad, he decided to fatten himself in Feke's pastures. Smibert was probably not the only London artist who had traded a precarious existence in a metropolis thick with competitors for the assurance of remunerative jobs in the New World. The prospect of making a living on only a meager talent had surely something to do with the temporary emigration of painters of limited talent to America in those years. Wollaston was another example and Mr. Burroughs quotes many more (*loc. cit.,* p. 54). The expectation that he might perchance step into Robert Feke's shoes may very well have occasioned Blackburn's venture. He stayed in Boston until 1761; the length of his stay goes to show that he had not planned just a flying trip, but that he had come for good. If the anticipation of remunerative jobs had been the chief reason for his coming, then it was only logical that he sounded retreat in the early 'sixties when Copley began to monopolize practically every portrait commission in town.

the rage around the middle of the century, first in France, next everywhere at the courts of Europe; I mean those masquerades known as "shepherd portraits." The likeness of *Mary Sylvester Dering* (Metropolitan Museum, Fig. 78), painted at about the same time as that of her sister, *Mrs. Cheseborough* (1754), was one of the earliest of its kind in America. Copley eventually painted *Ann Tyng Smelt* (Fig. 79) in a similar outfit, with the shepherd's crook, though not with the lamb. Afterwards he seems to have found how little such pastoral theatrics were in keeping with the American environment and abandoned them.

However, Blackburn was not a very skillful designer. The gawky distortion of the lower part of *Mrs. Cheseborough's* body plainly shows that the imitator of Hudson was incapable of approximating his master's sure and graceful drawing.[14] Nor was he at first a discerning observer of faces. A letter of 1757, published by Lawrence Park,[15] indicates that Blackburn drew his heads after some fixed pattern. His use of such superficial "short-cuts" was ominously matched by his lack of original feeling for roundness. It is significant that Feke's figures not only penetrated more deeply into space but were also psychologically more deep and penetrating than Blackburn's early portraits. Blackburn's portrait of *Mrs. Cheseborough* (Fig. 67) appears shallow beside Feke's *Mrs. Tench Francis* (Fig. 65), both in the literal and the metaphorical sense of the word.

What, then, was the outcome when Blackburn, trained and fairly mature, rubbed shoulders in Boston with Copley, who was relatively inexperienced and still in his teens? What that intercourse did to the art of both in the nine years after 1754 admits of two diametrically opposite interpretations. Either Copley's manner changed under the influence of Blackburn—which has been the accepted

[14]Alan Burroughs (*loc. cit.*, p. 57) points out that Blackburn went for advice to Joseph Badger when he was grappling with the representation of the feet in the portrait of *Governor Wentworth.*

[15]Reprinted by Alan Burroughs, *loc. cit.*, p. 55.

theory for a long time and seems natural considering Copley's youth and his colleague's experience; or Blackburn fell under the influence of Copley's "genius," who, no matter how young and untutored, made quite another fellow out of him. This latter theory, advanced as a possibility by Alan Burroughs, appears most reasonable, considering that certain qualities which distinguish Blackburn's paintings since 1756, and make them greatly superior to his earlier work, were natural to Copley and were latent in his likenesses from the very start, whereas no sign in Blackburn's early pictures predicted an eventual change from a facile technician to a serious student of human character.[16] Nor did the stiffness which marked his style from the beginning ever quite disappear from his mature work. It was still present in the portraits of *Sir Francis* and *Lady Bernard,* of 1760 (Hartford, Conn., Avery Memorial Gallery). Now, there is no doubt in my mind that what was progressive about Blackburn's astonishing likenesses of *Mr. and Mrs. Jonathan Simpson,* of 1758 (Boston Museum), stemmed from Copley; namely, the interpretation, the modelling, and the spatial freedom. Only the old-fashioned, stiff design, particularly the body carriage of *Mrs. Simpson* (Fig. 80), revealed the typical Blackburn.

The fact is noteworthy. To realize the full bearing it had on the growth of the American tradition, one need only remember to what extent in earlier periods even strong-willed New England painters used to fall under the thrall of every fifth-rate European. Copley was the first who refused to be such an easy mark. And beyond that, he was the first artist in America who molded the style of an English painter in the American tradition.

Still, the matter cannot be dismissed with a patriotic flourish. It is not as easy as all that. In the late seventeen-hundred-and-fifties Copley's likenesses of women also looked "prim and stiff"; compare the *Ann Tyng Smelt* (Fig. 79). And if his picture of *William Brattle* (Fig. 82) is seen side-by-side with Blackburn's *Joseph*

[16]Alan Burroughs, *loc. cit.*, pp. 56–57, gives a perfect analysis of Blackburn's evolution.

*Dwight* (Fig. 81)—both in similar attitudes, both with "speaking" right hands of identical design—and it is realized that these two pictures were painted in Boston in the same year, 1756—then, how is one to decide with certainty which painter has the claim to originality and which hasn't?

A critic prejudiced in favor of Blackburn may point to the clumsy contour of the *William Brattle* and, contrasting it with the smoother contour of the *Joseph Dwight,* may find that Copley had much to learn from the more elegant metropolitan visitor. A critic prejudiced in favor of Copley may point to the remarkable change of Blackburn's approach: in this instance he gave a rounded study of character, while only two years back his portraits were conventional and evinced no apparent interest in human psychology. Obviously, this change must be credited to the influence of Copley who alone in Boston had that particular slant, and already had it as a boy of sixteen when he painted the *Reverend William Welsteed.* In fact, a Copley partisan has more than that to offer in evidence of Copley's originality—or independence, if one prefers that word. Copley did not make *William Brattle* pose in the leisurely attitude of the *Joseph Dwight,* with the left arm rested on a lateral support—a formula which had gone to seed in the shops of the British portrait manufacturers of the school of Cheron and Vanderbanck. *William Brattle* stands erect, as the painter had seen men standing in the likenesses of Robert Feke.

But how, then, if one turns to a somewhat later stage in Copley's development and finds him vying with precisely those threadbare studio poses of the English school? The posture of *Benjamin Pickman* (1761, New York, Miss Edith Wetmore, Fig. 84) is not identical with that of Vanderbanck's *John Michael Rysbrack* (1728, London, National Portrait Gallery, Fig. 83), yet, judging by the general similarity in the rhythmical development of pose and proportions, it was floating before Copley's mind when he painted young *Mr. Pickman.* In other instances of the same period no doubt at all is left as to whence Copley's inspiration came. The *Epes Sargent* (*circa* 1760, New York, Mrs. Oswald W. Knauth, Fig. 86) is closely related to Joseph Highmore's *Gentleman in a Silk Vest* (painted *circa* 1745, Huntington Gallery, San Marino, Cal., Fig. 85); compare the postures and the tortuous patterns derived from them. Besides, Highmore's painting (which is, stylistically speaking, "later" than Vanderbanck's) helped Copley to a more advanced idea of voluminosity. I believe only since his greater familiarity with that English painter was "Copley's amplitude of feeling, even in such a detail as a nostril or an eyelid, distinct from Blackburn's small-mindedness, which attains at best only a miniature-like precision."[17]

Be this as it may. There is little reason to question that Blackburn functioned as an intermediary. One is compelled to assume that it was he who acquainted Copley through conversation and examples with what was going on in England, particularly in the studio of Thomas Hudson. Thence, for certain, came the excessive display of metallic-looking drapery, which it took Copley a long time to discard. In the *Mary and Elizabeth Royall* portrait (*circa* 1758, Boston, Museum of Fine Arts, Fig. 87), Copley piled up a veritable mountain range of satin as a pedestal under the two bust likenesses and elaborated this appendage until it was visually much more important than the likenesses themselves. Copley seems to have realized only slowly that his deference to a British convention (for which Hogarth had but ridicule) kept him from seeing ensembles, from correlating the parts and from putting the stress on what should be essentials in a portrait, namely, the head and the hands. It took years before his draperies ceased to stand out as something separate. The unity he ultimately achieved may be seen in the *Judge Martin Howard* (1767, Boston, Social Law Library, Fig. 88). Though the sitter wears a robe of very pronounced scarlet, it no longer stands out as a decorative addition or, for that matter, as

[17]Virgil Barker, *A Critical Introduction, loc. cit.*, p. 17.

"drapery" at all. The folds do not detract attention from the head and the hand because they are viewed as a part of the entire figure, the entire setting, and the entire illumination.

From about 1765 Copley began to throw overboard, one after another, the standards and conventions which so far had been handicaps, if not blinders, to him in the years of his association with Blackburn. The first thing to go was the ready-made attitude. Like ready-made clothes, it prevented the sitter from showing his true personality. Those fixed postures after Vanderbanck or Highmore were useful as long as Copley believed characterization could be obtained by assembling faithful records of faces, drapes, clothes and settings and by entering these records piecemeal into a preconceived formula. But the moment Copley realized that a full characterization could not be attained by such a method the standard poses were worthless. Characterization had to be worked out from the entire person—from *Gestalt,* as we would say. An individual's gait and bearing were at least as important as was the shape of his nose, the color of his eyes, and the texture of his skin. The way a woman sits in a chair, folds her hands in her lap or carries herself—all this he found to be more revealing than the proportions of her face or the measurement of her waistline.

This discovery was an incentive to the most significant reform in colonial portraiture. A new kind of exhaustive character depiction was made possible when the individual sitter's most personal pose was used for the basic motif and the entire composition of the canvas was derived from it. Copley's novel method accounts in a large measure for the unprecedented intimacy of his colonial portraits since 1765.

## IV. *The Consummation of the Colonial Tradition*

To evaluate the full measure of Copley's achievement, one must bear in mind that a likeness painter does not have nearly as many opportunities for novel compositions as a landscape or history painter. With one or two persons seated and standing, Copley had but a narrow range for an original spacing and grouping, an expressive flow of line and light, a rich variety of coloring, and so on. Considering these limitations of the portrait painter, his later likenesses reveal an amazing emancipation from rote and conventional monotony.

Every motif in them was fundamentally new. *Nathaniel Hurd* (*circa* 1765, Cleveland Museum, Fig. 89), leaning across the table with hands folded and the head tilted a little sidewards as in a momentary response to some remark that was just made; *The Boy with the Squirrel* (Fig. 90), suddenly relaxing the action of his right hand as he turns toward an imaginary interlocutor; and all those merchants, lawyers, townclerks, or schoolmasters–*Thomas* and *Nicholas Boylston, John Gardiner, Thomas Cary,* and *Ezekiel Goldthwaight*–caught in a split second as they were sitting at their desks or in their studies; jovial in manner, spirited in expression, informal in dress and behavior; swinging around on their chairs to greet the visitor, to converse with him, to lecture to him. The direct lifelikeness evoked by these informal arrangements is particularly striking when they are compared with the earlier likenesses for which the sitters were told to assume certain hackneyed studio attitudes.

The general appreciation that Copley's work of this period enjoys with the public centers on other values than the historian of colonial art finds necessary to point out. Every one of the portraits I have just mentioned has a place in the heart of the American people mainly because of the historic significance of the persons represented and also because of the finish given to every detail represented in them. One who loves Copley for such reasons does not want to be told that the treatment of space in these paintings signified such progress as colonial art had not experienced before. Yet, he must be told. For that progress counted immeasurably in the further evolution of the American tradition. The very pose of *Thomas Boylston* (Fogg Art Museum of Harvard University, Fig. 92) contributes to a constant ebb and flow of space values: the foreshortened posture undulating from the lower left foreground to the upper right distance; the full face fixed between the rearward slant of the shoulders and arms; the relative spacing of the hands—all this left Feke and Smibert far behind. It was as if Copley was not just one but several generations removed from them.

And if the public believes, as it still does, that the lifelikeness of Copley's late portraits results from the painter's neat elaboration of details, then it passes by the fundamental contribution which made Copley truly the classic of colonial portrait painting. The "life" that breathes forth from the most extraordinary of all his colonial likenesses, namely the *Mrs. Thomas Boylston* (1766, Fogg Art Museum of Harvard University, Fig. 5), springs not so much from the multitude and the elaboration of details as from the subordination of those details to the ensemble. What made Copley the classic of colonial art was his "large" apperception.

Copley could proceed with a scientist's scrutiny where details were indispensable to the interest of intimate and comprehensive characterization. Witness: the sensitive design and subtle modelling of Mrs. Boylston's face; her long-fingered bony hands, the left one in full light, the right one immersed in a melting shadow and fashioned out of strokes of gray and ruddy paint; the perfect illusion of the tulle on her shoulder and the grayish brown taffeta of her dress. Moreover, in addition to painting the venerable old lady, Copley painted a venerable old chair, a distinguished piece of family furniture which had been through at least as many adventures as its mistress. Through countless years of use, one of the depressions in its upholstered back, caused originally by the backstitch of the quilting thread, had developed into a sizeable bump. That bump was faithfully recorded. Perhaps it was prosaic to do that. But Copley's portraiture was prose fundamentally. And that little episode could not be left out of his painted biography of a veteran of Boylston family comfort. But the secret of Copley's mature "prose" is not to be disclosed by isolating its separate words and passages from the vigorous total construction to which they minister. The secret resides in Copley's subordination of intimate details to a spatial composition of great breadth, unity, and simplicity.

Like all indigenous colonial painters, Copley conceived of portraiture as a still-life proposition, even afterwards in England. But elaboration alone would not have signalled the rise from the early to the middle colonial style of which this portrait is an example. Copley gave its mature form to the older American tradition, in which he was bred, not by elaboration but by simplicity. He sacrificed what was entertaining and embellishing to what was structurally necessary. To what extent adornment was cleared away in order that the "architectural" structure of the whole should be strengthened and rendered articulate may be gleaned from a comparison with his portraits ten years earlier, for example, the *Ann Tyng Smelt* (Fig. 79), with all her display of winsome attributes.

In *Mrs. Boylston's* portrait, Copley harnessed every means of design and lighting in order to produce, literally and figuratively speaking, the impression of a "fully rounded" personality. The painter's symbol for that is space occupied by cohesive volume; volume freely expanding in three dimensions. His efforts were not always crowned with the same success, as is evidenced by the more cramped likeness of *Mrs. Robert Hooper* of Marblehead (1767, New York Public Library, Fig. 91). Mrs. Boylston's movement is more liquid, and the space in which she appears is likewise more liquid. Her whole being seems immersed in atmosphere.

The journey to England and across Europe, both going to and returning from Rome, in 1774 and 1775, spelled the temporary termination of the colonial tradition as regards Copley personally and painting in America in general. The event and its consequences bear sufficient weight to warrant the question: Did this happen only because of the trivial incidents that I pointed out earlier in this chapter? Was Copley's marriage to the daughter of the tory, Richard Clarke, alone responsible for his desertion?

We may rest assured: Copley wouldn't have stayed in the colonies anyway. In the late 'sixties he had so outgrown the modest standards of colonial art that he was a solitary. The creator of the high colonial tradition was its only representative. It takes more than human strength and self-denial for an ambitious artist to endure such isolation. Years before his marriage he was getting tired of conditions in Boston. In one of his letters to his brother Henry he described himself as "peculiarly unlucky in living in a place into which there has not been one portrait brought within my memory that is worthy to be called a picture." To him it was "not a little mortifying" that the people regarded painting "no more than any other useful trade, as they sometimes term it, like that of a carpenter, tailor, or shoemaker, not as one of the most noble arts in the world." Moreover, he was anxious to improve by competing with painters who were his betters. Such were not to be found in the colonies. "Boston," as Trumbull's father afterwards said of Connecticut, "was not Athens." It was backwoodish. Surely, Copley had made progress. He had broken away from the primitive colonial manner. But what now? He wanted to see and learn more. He was not afraid of other artists' *finesse* as Smibert was who had run away from London to New England to be at the top of lesser men.

Besides, Copley was lured to England step by step. Already *The Boy with the Squirrel* had established his reputation abroad. On September 2, 1766, Copley had been elected Fellow of the Society of Artists of Great Britain. Sir Joshua Reynolds let him know through Captain Bruce that "with the advantages of the example and instruction which he could have in Europe" the future would belong to Copley, "provided you could receive these aids before it was too late in life and before your manner and taste were corrupted or fixed by working in your own little way in Boston." At the same time Benjamin West was inviting him to stay at his house in London. Two years before his marriage and seven before his actual departure, Copley was weighing the pros and cons. It was all very difficult to decide. The financial risk was incalculable. In Boston he had "arrived." Would he in London make anything near the sums he needed to keep up the lavish standards of living to which he was slowly getting accustomed in Boston? By 1767 he had decided to go for two years and, if he failed, to return baffled to America. Then, however, he did not want to leave his ailing mother.

At least he would not grow stale in Boston. If it could not be England now, let it at least be New York or Philadelphia. Copley went to both places in 1771. He received plenty of commissions in New York. In Philadelphia, in the house of William Allen, he saw for the first time a larger collection of foreign paintings, most of them replicas. One, in fact, after Correggio, was painted by Benjamin West. His descriptions of Titian's and Correggio's work in letters to Henry Pelham were enthusiastic. It gave him a premonition of what was in store for him in Florence and Rome.

Once more he returned to Boston. But the town was becoming tense with political strife. The time was ripe. Leaving his mother, wife, and child behind, he embarked for London in June, 1774.

Only a chauvinist could have lamented that Copley did not stay for the benefit of American art. Copley could not see anything meritorious in remaining an *American* painter. Wasn't America in those pre-revolutionary days just another part of England? So why not get all the advantages of English culture that could be obtained? In the end the colonies would be thankful when Copley returned after a few years. But he never returned. We shall find another Copley in Rome and in London. To comprehend the change it is necessary first to turn to Benjamin West.

# CHAPTER FIVE

# BENJAMIN WEST

## I. *West in Rome*

BENJAMIN WEST, from Chester County, Pennsylvania, rose to the highest rank that an artist could attain in England. He was President of the Royal Academy, the successor to Sir Joshua Reynolds. He was revered as a God-inspired genius. Visitors to his home uncovered before his paintings and were moved to tears when the master spoke to them. He died in the belief that his art was immortal. His funeral was conducted in the Cathedral of Saint Paul in the presence of three Dukes, two Marquises, nine Earls, an Archbishop, four Bishops, and the Lord Mayor.[1] John Galt, in his biography of West, expressed the general opinion of the connoisseurs: "His name will be classed with Michael Angelo and Raphael. As the former has been compared to Homer and the latter to Virgil, in Shakespeare we shall perhaps find the best likeness to the genius of Mr. West." Of course, there were also a few dissenters. But Lord Byron's fling at "the dotard West, Europe's worst daub, poor England's best" was, as usual, an anticipation of what later generations were to think rather than a reflection of the common contemporary opinion. What we now think of West has been epitomized by William T. Whitley: "He was a bad painter but a good man."

How was it possible that an artist of such mediocre talent could win international fame—an American at that? For when West came to England, no American painter's name had been heard of outside the borders of the colonies. The answer is that art was evaluated

[1]William T. Whitley, *Art in England, 1800–1820,* Cambridge (University Press), 1928, p. 306.

and measured in West's day, at least among erudite connoisseurs, by other standards than are valid today and that his peculiar inclination and training were admirably suited to those standards. To comprehend this, we must examine his training as well as the vagaries of European art in the last third of the eighteenth century.

When Benjamin West graduated from Pennsylvania College at the age of eighteen, he had obtained what was considered at the time the education of a classical scholar. That is to say, his head was crammed with Homer, Virgil and Ovid, but his spelling was so deficient that newspapermen in London afterwards sarcastically remarked "the President of the Academy is a scholar who must think before he writes."[2] His artistic education was just as unsound. He could neither paint nor draw properly, but his instructor, William Williams, had fed his mind with the *Theory of Painting* and other æsthetic treatises of Jonathan Richardson—indoctrinated contemplations operating with cut-and-dried categories, as are implied in their cumbersome titles, *e.g., The Connoisseur, an essay on the whole art of Criticism as it relates to Painting, and a discourse on the Dignity, Certainty, Pleasure and Advantage of the science of a connoisseur.*

At the age of twenty-two, West went to Italy for study. When he arrived in Rome, in 1760, he flung himself wholeheartedly into the arms of the three men whom Europe at that time hailed as *restauratori del arte,* the antiquarian Johann Jakob Winckelmann, and the painters Anton Raphael Mengs and Pompeo Battoni. They were preaching a new ideal of art. It was laid down in Winckelmann's *Reflections on the Imitation of the Paintings and Sculptures of the Greeks* (1756) and in Mengs' *Concerning Beauty and Taste in Painting* (1762). West was familiar with the core of the new theory from Ten Kate's *Le Beau Idéal* which served as preface to Richardson's *Account of the Statues and Basreliefs, Drawings, and Pictures in Italy,* a guidebook which every educated traveller used to

[2]W. T. Whitley, *Art in England, 1800–1820, op. cit.*, p. 54.

take with him on his Italian tour. Only one thing was news to West, that this ideal art was infallible and, therefore, subject to no change of taste.

What these "Classicists" taught was eclecticism, and, if one overlooked its gross fallacies, the theory of eclecticism proved that perfect beauty could be derived from certain authorities. The theory, as expounded by Mengs, boils down to this: Beauty is something absolute; it is the "idea" of the perfect form. Therefore Beauty cannot be found in the multitude of impure forms that are nature. Pure beauty, however, may be selected from nature's impurity. It has been the merit of a few truly great artists of the past to have done that selecting. Throughout the ages, they have selected the parts that are perfect and so they have brought mankind nearer and nearer to knowing the ideal. Classicism, then, must carry selection farther. If the *most* perfect parts are selected from the perfect parts that have been already selected in the past, then art must be brought still nearer to ideal beauty. It follows that it is a waste of time to cope with raw nature. The artist's business is not with nature, but with Antiquity, with Raphael, and with the other classic artists who have achieved the preliminary selection of the beautiful parts from nature. But what remains to be done is to assemble into a perfect whole the perfect parts they have selected. And here is the way it must be done: Polykletus and other Greeks selected the most perfect postures of man and the most beautiful proportions of man's body; therefore, artist, take your postures and proportions from Polykletus and the Greeks. Raphael selected the most perfect design and the most beautiful composition; therefore, artist, take your design and compositions from Raphael. Correggio's chiaroscuro is more perfect than any other painter's; therefore, add Correggio's chiaroscuro to Greek proportions and postures as well as to Raphael's design and composition. Add to this the coloration of Titian, for no more perfect colorist can be found. In short, roll the perfect parts of Polykletus, Raphael, Correggio, and Titian into one and you will have the perfections of each multiplied by four. That was the cookbook of common sense. There was a recipe for every work of art. Academicians of the period were so convinced of the wisdom of this that they warned teachers and students not to invent original pictures, but rather to copy the beautiful parts in old masters' tableaux.[3]

The eclecticism of Mengs, Battoni, and the rest was the twin brother of the philosophy of common sense; it descended from the lofty classicism of Nicolas Poussin as the philosophy of enlightenment descended from the rationalism of Descartes. In their respective fields of art and thought, Poussin and Descartes had sought to approximate the finality of pure mathematics. Descartes, by deducting Knowledge from reason alone; Poussin, by deducting Beauty from reason alone. The methods of classicistic art and rationalistic philosophy were founded on the hypothesis of certain supreme and infallible principles. Poussin's dogmas were Ancient Art and Raphael. These were absolute perfection; whosoever dared to question their validity was either a fool or a criminal. "The only certain road to the sublime is the study of Antiquity, Raphael and Domenichino."[4] In London, Reynolds defended "an artificial style of the highest degree" on the ground that any grand style presupposes, on the part of the spectator, a cultivated and artificial state of mind.[5] When he was accused of plagiarisms for having borrowed attitudes from ancient masters, Horace Walpole came to his defense: "Not only candour but criticism must deny the force of the charge. When a single posture is imitated from an historic picture and applied to a portrait in a different dress and with new attributes, this is not plagiarism, but quotation: and a quotation from a great author,

[3]See the directions that Vien, head of the French Academy in Rome, received from his boss in Paris; reprinted in Jean Locquin, *La peinture d'histoire en France,* Paris, 1912, p. 98.

[4]Letter of Menagot to Angiviller, head of all French Art Schools, of January, 1788, published in Jean Locquin, *op. cit.,* p. 100.

[5]*Discourse XV*. For the whole matter see Edgar Wind: *Humanitätsidee und heroisiertes Portrait in der englischen Kultur des 18ten Jahrhunderts* (Vorträge der Bibliothek Warburg), Leipzig, 1932.

with a novel application of the sense, has always been allowed to be an instance of parts and taste; and may have more merit than the original."[6]

That was eclecticism in the platitudinizing age of enlightenment. In it creative genius did not have a place any more than miracles had in the Scriptures. Artistic spontaneity and inspiration were superstitions. Genius was a luxury. Said Sir Joshua: "Nothing is denied to well-directed industry." To prove that what he said was true, Reynolds might have pointed to Mengs, Battoni and West as living examples.

The father of Mengs had "whipped art into the infant." When the son had been launched as a child prodigy he was compelled to spend his adolescent years secluded in the *Stanze* of the Vatican copying Raphael's frescoes from morning to night. After such sterile drudgery he emerged, in 1761, with a "creation" of his own: a ceiling picture for the villa of the Cardinal Albani representing *Apollo and the Muses on Mount Parnassus* (Fig. 93). Far from taking umbrage at the fact that this was a flimsy imitation of Raphael's *Mount Parnassus* fresco, every one was agreed that its "composite style of excellence" outranked Raphael's. For it was stuffed with additional classic postures and figures most of which were garnered from ancient marbles in the Papal collection. Artists flocked from the four corners of the world to study this absurd compilation. Two years after its completion Winckelmann solemnly dedicated his *History of the Art of Antiquity* "to Art, to this Age, and especially to Anton Raphael Mengs."

Pompeo Battoni was more a painter than a philosopher of art, yet his œuvre of eclectic paintings and drawings was but another illustration of the success of "well-directed industry."

Benjamin West was certainly better equipped with that article than he was with genius. And is it not evident why eclecticism should have fitted him so admirably? Here was a short cut to Beauty, a mechanical method by which absolute perfection could

[6]Horace Walpole, *Anecdotes* (1849) I, p. xvii.

be obtained without much talent, and an unfailing guarantee against criticism from the connoisseurs.

## II. *West in London*

In 1763 West left Italy freighted with all the wisdom of the eclectic savants and established himself in London. The work which made him famous, *The Death of General Wolfe at Quebec* (Ottawa, National Gallery, Fig. 94), was a wholesale endorsement of the eclectic school. It was exhibited in 1771, but may have been in the making since 1764, when West painted the portrait of *General Monckton,* who was General Wolfe's first lieutenant in 1758.

Had not West's indifferent painting been afterwards considered the epitome of the historic school, it would not have been wreathed with myths and legends which still lend to it a significance that it does not deserve.[7] Let these spurious wreaths be removed before the picture is approached.

John Galt made up a story that was accepted and spread far and wide by William Dunlap. This is the story: When Sir Joshua inspected the canvas, he was shocked to find that West had painted the British soldiers in their actual uniforms. But after West explained that Quebec was located in a region unknown to Greeks and Romans and that the battle was fought at a time when warriors did not wear the costume of antiquity, Reynolds surrendered with these words: "West has conquered. He has treated the subject as it ought to be treated. I retract my objections. I foresee that this picture will not only become one of the most popular, but will occasion a revolution in art."[8] Inasmuch as the story comes from the un-

[7]Edgar Wind, *The Revolution of History Painting* (Journal of the Warburg Institute, II, 1938, pp. 116 ff.), still believes "it is *recorded* that Reynolds tried to dissuade West from committing so flagrant a breach of academic rules," and, after adding Copley to West, concludes that "the final breach with the Academic rules of history painting was produced by an impact of democratic ideas proclaimed by a group of American artists." (*Ibid.,* p. 126.)

[8]Dunlap's *History, op. cit.,* I, p. 67.

trustworthy Galt, it is shaky enough as it is. But since its content is out of keeping with known facts, it is high time that it be dismissed as completely unfounded.

To begin with, West was not the first to paint *The Death of Wolfe*. The subject had been fashionable in London when West was still in Rome. In 1763, George Romney sent in a picture of the same title to the Society of British Artists in the hope of winning one of the prizes that had been offered for the best historical paintings submitted.[9] In the following year, Edward Penny exhibited another *Death of Wolfe* in the Society of Artists. "Apropos of Penny's *Death of Wolfe* in which the soldiers are in British uniforms," remarked Mr. C. H. Collins Baker in 1933, "it should be recognized that this preceded by seven years West's more famous *Death of Wolfe* which is generally credited with having been the first picture to break the tradition of painting modern soldiers in classical costume."[10] Since Penny was a charter member of the Royal Academy, of which Sir Joshua was the first president, it may be taken for granted that Reynolds (1) knew that West was not the first to "break the rules" and (2) never said that West's painting would "occasion a revolution." It has been usual for earlier historians to confirm the "daring innovation" of West by pointing out that five years after West's picture was exhibited James Barry still painted *The Death of Wolfe* "so classical in treatment that it represented a combat of naked men." This has also been disproved. In 1928 William Thomas Whitley published a description of Barry's picture from the *Public Advertiser* in which a naval officer, a midshipman, and two grenadiers were expressly mentioned. "How," asks Mr. Whitley, "could the reporter have identified naval officers and grenadiers if all the combatants were nude?"[11]

It is curious that William Dunlap should have accepted this

[9] W. T. Whitley, *Artists and Their Friends in England, op. cit.*, I, p. 191.
[10] C. H. Collins Baker, *British Painting*, Boston, 1933, p. 95.
[11] W. T. Whitley, *Artists and Their Friends in England, op. cit.*, I, p. 376.

fiction on the authority of Galt, whom he publicly branded as "a most injudicious biographer." Dunlap dismissed most of "the puerilities of his performance and the absurd tales and speeches of general officers, Quaker preachers, Indian actors, and Italian *improvisatori* as altogether unworthy."[12] The only plausible reason for his adopting this particular legend is that it seemed designed to make an American the father of realistic English history painting and *The Death of Wolfe* its ancestral monument.

West's picture did not "occasion a revolution" any more than did his seven other pictures that were jointly exhibited in 1771—four classical and three biblical subject paintings. The painter made no conscious effort to record what happened at Quebec, though he was well informed about the details of the battle through his personal friend, General Monckton. West painted an Indian warrior and portraits of the officers who participated in the fight. But none of these "realistic" details can free the painter of the charge that his picture is a typical example of eclectic construction, in fact, a compilation. It is not derived from Poussin, as Mr. Collins Baker thinks; it is derived from Raphael. The central group surmounted by the flag was taken from the *Holy Family Canigiani* (Munich, Alte Pinakothek, Fig. 96); the group on the left, including the Indian brave, harks back to the main group in the left-hand foreground of *The School of Athens* (Fig. 95). The classicist Canova hit the nail on the head when he told Haydon: "West does not 'compose'; he groups models."[13]

As an historian I find myself in a dilemma. Do the importance and influence which West enjoyed in his day and age carry the obligation for me to discuss his entire œuvre and so to contribute to my reader's boredom? Or does the fact that he was the exponent of a period which forfeited "art" for questionable "theories" relieve me from such exhaustive and tedious scrutiny? I am resolved to

[12]Dunlap's *History, op. cit.*, I, p. 33.
[13]W. T. Whitley, *Art in England, 1800–1820, op. cit.*, p. 252.

dismiss completeness where the general topic of the book does not call for it and to select only a few characteristic works of West for intensive discussion.

As a portraitist West was *quantité négligeable,* though the more lenient of his critics are inclined to see real merit in his painted likenesses. West himself thought differently: "I seldom paint portraits," he told Archibald Robertson, "and when I do I neither please myself nor my employers."[14] West who, like his biographer Galt, "had no taste for the blemishes of mankind" was quite insensitive to characterization. He could not enspirit either his sitters or his descriptive media. His hand did not vibrate, and his color did not glow more warmly in response to any emotional reaction. In lieu of painterly characterization, West often resorted to the tricks of the "historic style" which Oliver Goldsmith satirized in the fourteenth chapter of *The Vicar of Wakefield.*

"If a portrait painter is desirous to raise and improve a subject," advised Sir Joshua in his fourth *Discourse,* "he has no other means than by approaching it to a general idea." The manner is familiar from Sir Joshua's Three Misses Montgomery as *The Graces, Decorating Hymen,* and *Miss Sarah Siddons as the Tragic Muse* guarded on her throne by Pity and Terror. The chief trick was to load the portrait with allegory. West may have felt reminded of old Jonathan Richardson's axiom that what made a painter great was spiritual invention; but he did not have the imagination of Reynolds. The best he could do was the absurd *Alderman Sawbridge,* of 1772 (Fig. 98), clothed as a Roman Tribune, *Lady Beauchamps Proctor* decorating Hymen, of 1778 (Fig. 97), or *The Drummond Family* (1766, Minneapolis Art Institute, Fig. 99) joined in memory with a deceased ancestor whose likeness they are contemplating; eventually George Romney's *Beaumont Family* (London, National Gallery) made this sentimental thought rather popular.

His ecclesiastic and secular history subjects are historically important inasmuch as they contributed substantially to the uprooting

[14] W. T. Whitley, *Gilbert Stuart, op. cit.,* p. 42.

of the colonial tradition. But beyond the methods employed in their invention and composition they need not concern us. All of them were made to be read rather than seen. They were shallow "painted literature." As has been realized long ago, they had "neither style nor sincerity"[15] or, as Hazlitt said, they were "only great by the acre."[16]

My selection of a few examples is made somewhat more easy by the circumstance that a great number of this class of paintings has vanished to heaven knows where. Some were removed when the walls that they adorned were torn down. This is true of all of West's murals and of many of his painted windows for St. George's Hall and the Collegiate Church at Windsor, for St. Paul's at Birmingham, and for Fonthill Abbey, the fancy-Gothic church that was erected in the late 'nineties of the eighteenth century. Others have survived as engravings and are now enjoying undisturbed peace in the folders of the Print Room of the British Museum; for instance, the silly allegories of *The Arts and Sciences,* exhibited in 1790 as decorations for Queen's Lodge, Windsor. Nor do his altarpieces for St. Stephen at Wallbrook, St. Paul's Cathedral in London, Trinity Chapel in Cambridge, Winchester Cathedral, and Greenwich Hospital hold any interest for us. His extant easel pictures are for the most part locked up in the storerooms of the museums that own them; only few of them are occasionally shown, for example, the enormous canvases for the Pennsylvania Hospital, *Death on the Pale Horse*[17] and *Christ Rejected by Caiaphas,*[18] and

[15]Samuel Isham, *loc. cit.*, p. 58.

[16]W. T. Whitley, *Art in England, 1800–1820, op. cit.*, p. 225.

[17]The Pennsylvania Academy owns the original (dated 1817) and an oil sketch which was exhibited at The Paris *Salon* of 1802. The earliest sketch (1796) belongs to Lord Leconfield. A drawing of the whole is in the Royal Academy at London.

[18]A first sketch was exhibited in Paris (1802), the finished canvas in London (1814). This was shipped to Philadelphia in 1817. *A Select Group of Five Plates* representing separate heads of the painting, engraved, from drawings by Henry Corbould, by Edward Scriven, was published in July, 1814.

the pictures for Alderman Boydell's *Shakespeare Gallery,* particularly the scenes from Lear and Hamlet.[19]

As good an example of West's ancient History Pieces as could be found is the one with the long-winded title *Erasistratus the Physician Discovers the Love of Antiochus for Stratonice* (Fig. 100). It was exhibited for the first time in London in 1775. The theme had been very popular on the French stage, since early in the seventeenth century.[20]

The subject, an anticipation of the *Tristan and Iseult* motif, was taken from Plutarch's "Life of Demetrius Poliorketes": Prince Antiochus is passionately in love with his stepmother Stratonice. He resolves that the only honorable solution of his problem is to starve himself to death. Erasistratus, the physician, recognizes the young man's love-sickness from its symptoms: His patient is indifferent to all the fair ladies at court except Stratonice. Whenever she visits her stepson in the company of his father, Seleucus, the prince shows alarming symptoms—he perspires, his voice falters, and the action of his heart and pulse are irregular. (Plutarch was quite specific, probably because he was here describing the foremost physician of the Hellenistic epoch—the earliest known nerve-and-heart specialist.) The story has a happy ending: Seleucus abdicates the crown, Antiochus is proclaimed king, and Stratonice becomes his queen.

The nearly one hundred and fifty years that have elapsed since West completed his picture have removed us so completely from the then valid type of "history painting" that we are at a loss how to approach that sort of picture. The nineteenth century, with its

[19]*The Mad Scene,* once owned by Robert Fulton, is in the Boston Museum, *The Meeting of Cordelia and Lear,* in the Huntington Gallery, San Marino, Cal. (Fig. 103). *Ophelia and Laertes,* mentioned by Harriet Martineau as "the preposterous picture in the home of Nicholas Longworth," is now in the Cincinnati Museum of Art.

[20]Louis Sorieri, *Boccaccio's Story of Tito e Gisippo in European Literature,* New York (Comparative Literature Series, Institute of French Studies of Columbia University), 1937, pp. 132 ff.

stress on psychological veracity, has made it next to impossible for us to appreciate West's stilted manner of expression. If we wish to do him justice at all, we should remember that "truthfulness," both physical and psychological, did not count with the eclectic classicists. *"Qu'importe la vérité si les attitudes sont nobles!"* was the reply of Jacques Louis David to a critic who objected that his pictorial oratory did not ring true.

There was not an original thought in the picture (Fig. 100). Besides purloining certain figures from Gavin Hamilton's *Andromache lamenting Hector,* of 1764,[21] West took for his model at least one, perhaps several, versions of the subject.[22] Certainly he followed the *Stratonice* (Fig. 101) that won the Rome Prize for young Jacques Louis David in 1774. A comparison of the two works is revealing, inasmuch as it helps us to gauge West's weaknesses.

[21]Reproduced in Jean Locquin, *loc. cit.,* Plate X.

[22]West's connection with the doctrines of eclectic classicism will be further clarified by following back the story of this particular subject-piece to its origin. *Seleucus renouncing Stratonice,* one of several similar paintings by Gerard de Lairesse, was described at great length in Winckelmann's *Gedanken über die Nachahmung der griechischen Werke in der Malerey und Bildhauerkunst* (ed. 1756, pp. 76–80). In fact, it was there proclaimed as "deserving to be numbered among the finest works of the world." Another canvas, *The Love-sick Prince,* runs like a *leitmotif* through Goethe's *Wilhelm Meisters Lehrjahre* (1777–96). A painting similar to the one described in that famous German novel (VIII: 10), the work of the Venetian, Andrea Celesti (*ante* 1706, Cassel, Picture Gallery), seems to have inspired the *Stratonice* of J. L. David (1774, Ecole des Beaux Arts; sketch in the Chéramy Collection). In the same year James Barry painted and exhibited the subject. Perhaps West was familiar not only with David's prize painting, but also with Pompeo Battoni's composition (Berlin, Private Collection) and the picture by Januarius Zick (Wiesbaden, Municipal Museum, Fig. 102); both more or less resemble West's version. There can be no doubt as to his having known David's composition; it attracted wide attention shortly before West contemplated his large canvas. Another smaller composition by West, showing only six characters in a tent-like setting and arranged quite differently, is in the Worcester Art Museum. Evidence of West's familiarity with David's painting resides not in similarities of stage-set and properties so much—these had become traditional iconography in the course of time—as in other analogies which may hardly be considered accidental. In each picture eleven figures are similarly grouped.

David's expression was lucid. What he said he said forcefully and with a sense of dramatic progression that registered with the beholder. In his picture, the elements of the plot were visually comprehensible even if one did not know the literary details. The accusing gesture of the physician, the embarrassment of the woman whom he points out, and the prince rising toward her as in a wave of yearning—these essentials, related to each other by an arch that spans the width of the canvas, were at once visually eloquent. The beholder's eyes also sensed the dramatic clashing of the two movements that proceed in opposite directions: the physician's arm was flung from the left in the teeth of the crowd that entered from the right. Within those moving masses, protagonists were distinguished from the chorus; in fact, the praise that Winckelmann lavished on Gerard de Lairesse applied quite as well to David: "Characterization is distributed with such astuteness among the several characters that one character seems to enhance the plasticity of the other." David grouped the leading characters as two and two, putting Antiochus and Stratonice in the full light and shrouding Erasistratus and Seleucus in the dark.

West did not possess David's dramatic instinct nor could he narrate as lucidly in pictorial terms. In his picture there was neither emphasis nor subordination. There was hardly any difference between soloists and choir, nor grouping by the contrast of light and dark. Unless the beholder knew the text he was unable to tell what was supposed to be going on, or even that something particularly dramatic was going on. All the figures move in the same direction —in the direction of Stratonice's entrance. Want of precision left some gestures unexplained. What on earth was the meaning of Stratonice's gesticulation? Other histrionics were too obvious; this was especially painful when they were redundant, as the physician's, who felt the patient's pulse with one hand and his heart with the other; David had cleverly subordinated the pulse-taking to the exclamatory gesture of the physician's other hand. West's design was as vague as his stage direction. None of his contours registered optically the way David's did. How sluggish was the action of the prince's head! West's line had nothing of the swing of David's line. His voice did not resound as David's; it mumbled.

Throughout the sixty years of his career West did not, of course, continue to adhere to the doctrines of classicism as rigorously as he did in the sixties and seventies. He was influenced by the early romantic reaction of Stothard and Blake, but was too old to accept the new trend in full; after all, its instigators were thirty years his juniors. Still, it should be acknowledged that he bowed to Gainsborough's and Wilson's revival of landscape and that he gave valuable advice to young John Constable.

In course of time the extreme restraint of classicism was superseded by a more passionate movement, flinty design by painterly warmth, symmetry by less regular arrangements of figures and light. The rigid construction of *Erasistratus the Physician,* in terms of vertical and horizontal directions, was loosened up eighteen years later. In *Cordelia making herself known to King Lear* (Fig. 103) diagonals were allowed to predominate and the relief-like alignment of figures and background in parallel planes, that had been the rule with classicism, was superseded by an orientation from a point in the left-hand foreground to one in the right-hand distance. Furthermore, the uniform neutral brightness of the early picture, which rendered the outlines knife-edged and the modelling of the figures cold as polished marble, gave way to the glowing clair-obscure in which the romantic school liked to veil all things. Within another twenty years *Death on the Pale Horse,* a "five-acre" by-product of the apocalyptic subjects for Fonthill Abbey, was conceived in terms of complete asymmetry. A mass of brightness bursts from the distance on the extreme left; a mass of darkness burdens the foreground on the extreme right.

No less clearly than by his changing manner of composition West's bent for romanticism was revealed in his selection of subject matter. He had not been in London ten years when he began to prefer topics of medieval history to the classical ones. Although the one-time disciple of Mengs and Battoni never wholly abandoned classical themes, it is quite evident from the catalogues of his annual exhibitions at the Royal Academy, if they are scanned with a statistician's eyes, that classical histories, medieval histories, and landscapes succeeded each other chronologically in clearly marked periods.[23] Ultimately, as I have just said, landscape, the favorite vehicle of romantic expression, was accorded equal rights with figure subjects.[24]

But to the end West continued the practice of derivative acquisition of motifs. The *King Lear* pictures borrowed as heavily from Domenichino and Reni as *The Death of Wolfe* had borrowed from Raphael. Edgar, coiled as a madman in the right-hand foreground of *The Madscene from King Lear* (1793, Boston, Museum of Fine Arts), stemmed from one of Domenichino's Evangelists in the spandrels of the cupola of St. Andrea della Valle in Rome. The figure of Amor in the allegory-laden *Amor vincit omnia* (1811, Metropolitan Museum) reminds me of certain manneristic inventions of Guido Reni, for instance *Samson triumphant,* the picture in the Pinacotheca of Bologna.

It is significant that in this one regard West never changed. He never abandoned the method he had embraced in Rome. He was aware of the contempt of younger artists, such as William Blake,

[23]During the first three exhibitions (1769–1771) West's historical subjects were exclusively culled from antiquity; to wit, *Regulus departs from Rome, Leonidas, Hannibal, Venus and Adonis, Hector and Andromache, The Death of Procris.* The first romantic subjects appeared in 1773 alongside an equal number of ancient themes; to wit, *The Cave of Despair* (from "The Faerie Queen") and *Death of Chevalier Bayard.* Two years later West's interest in antiquity began to decline. *Erasistratus the Physician,* of 1775, was followed by no other classical subject piece until five years later and thereafter by none for a dozen years. Instead, West painted English medieval histories: *Alfred III, King of Mercia* (1778) and the *King Lear* pictures for Alderman Boydell (since 1789).

[24]Three landscapes were exhibited in 1796; to wit, *Harvest Scene, Landscape with Woodcutter, Washing the Sheep.* In 1799 he showed *The Bath of Venus,* "a poetic landscape."

who claimed that what made an artist great was his original vision. But West remained true to his first love—eclecticism.

Benjamin West left America when he was barely of age and never returned to the land of his birth. The evolution of his art in England would therefore be uninteresting to students of American art had it not influenced West's numerous American students who entered his school at various periods of time and carried back to the United States whatever happened to be his manner or his ideal at the time. With fresh students coming steadily to his "American Academy" from 1764 to 1811, the range of his influence was enormous, particularly in its duration. His first American pupil, Matthew Pratt, was born in 1734, his last American pupil, Samuel F. B. Morse, lived until 1872.

West's fatal influence molded three generations of artists. The first generation of students came in the 'sixties; these were men nearly of his own age: Matthew Pratt, Abraham Delancey, and Charles Wilson Peale. The second generation came in the 'seventies and early 'eighties; they were from fifteen to thirty years younger than West: Ralph Earl, Gilbert Stuart, John Trumbull, Mather Brown, Robert Fulton, and William Dunlap. As to age, the members of the third generation—his students during the first decade of the nineteenth century—might have been his grandsons. The oldest of them, Rembrandt Peale, was forty years younger than the master; his father had been West's student thirty years before. Washington Allston, Edward G. Malbone, Samuel Waldo and Morse were even younger.

These three generations brought the manner of Benjamin West to America. It was a manner completely out of joint with the colonial tradition which Copley had brought to its crest before he went to Italy. But meanwhile Copley himself had fallen into the British trap.

## CHAPTER SIX

# COPLEY IN EUROPE

### I. *Copley in Rome*

UNTIL he was forty years of age, Copley did not know more of the art of Europe than one knows of a poem of which a few words and passages, torn from their original context and jumbled by oral transmission, have been accidentally preserved. All his information was second-hand. It came to him from prints and a few poor replicas. All he knew of antiquity was Smibert's casts. All he knew of van Dyck was the head that Smibert had "lifted" from the full-length *Cardinal Bentivoglio* (Fig. 54). All he knew of Raphael was Smibert's copy of the *Madonna dell' Impannata* and a mezzotint reproduction of "a sweet picture of the Virgin with Jesus, over the chimney" in his stepfather's house.[1] Not until he visited the home of Chief Justice Allen in Philadelphia, in 1771, did he see other pictures of the renaissance in reproductions. There he got the first taste of Correggio from the replica of *Il Giorno* painted by Benjamin West.

Until he arrived in Rome, he had never attempted a picture with more than one full-length figure in it. The conversation piece of *Mr. and Mrs. Ralph Izard* (1775, Boston, Museum of Fine Arts, Fig. 109), wealthy people from South Carolina who resided in Rome, was his first essay in "composition"; that is, if we discount a puerile experiment, the *Mars, Venus, and Vulcan* (at one time in Bridgewater, Mass., Chapman Collection, Fig. 105), which he compiled from prints when he was seventeen.[2] Throughout his colonial

[1]Martha B. Amory, *Domestic and Artistic Life of John Singleton Copley,* Boston, 1882, p. 38.

[2]The painting has been discussed by William Rankin in the *Burlington Magazine,* VIII (London, 1906), pp. 68 f. Paintings in the same taste and of similar arrangement, like Pompeo Battoni's *Venus shows to Æneas the weapons forged*

period, Copley thought of "composition" as of some foreign problem insurmountable to an untutored fellow like himself. It was only when he got to London, before going to Italy, that he could speak of "a great difficulty removed from my mind. . . . I find the means by which composition is attained easier than I thought it had been." Small wonder that once he got to Rome he approached the monuments of antiquity and the paintings of the renaissance awe-stricken and bewildered. Many an opinion has been voiced by admirers of Raphael's *School of Athens,* but none quite so elementary as Copley's: "It has a kind of groundplan."[3]

The Rome to which Copley came in the summer of 1774 was no longer the city it had been when West had left eleven years earlier. Numerically, the ranks of the classicists had increased, but its disciples were beginning to emancipate themselves from the chilly ideology of Winckelmann, who was dead, and Mengs, who had gone to Madrid. James Barry, a classicist to the core, was preparing a treatise in which he violently attacked Winckelmann's theories;

*by Vulcan* (Vienna, Liechtenstein Gallery, done twenty-four years later), were not to be seen in New England; but engravings after paintings, and engraved bookplates, were probably to be found in Peter Pelham's engraver's shop. Gaspar de Crayer's *Hercules at the Crossroads,* engraved by Philippe Trière (reproduced as Fig. 56 in Erwin Panofsky, *Hercules am Scheidewege* (Leipzig, 1930), evinces some resemblance with Copley's painting as regards the whole as well as a number of striking details. It is likely that the print from which Copley made the drawing for his painting will be found in some French book. Even a superficial perusal of what eighteenth-century bookplates were accessible to me (of somewhat later date) has brought to light a number of like figures and compositions. At random I quote: *Les Amans Magnifiques,* and *Prologues de Psiché,* from the Molière edition illustrated by Boucher (1734); a plate showing Medea in the clouds, from the plates of *Le Toison d'Or,* in Vol. VII of the twelve-volume edition of *Le Théâtre de Pierre Corneille,* Geneva, 1764 (Fig. 104); another plate from the illustrations of *Medea,* in Vol. I of the same edition. For the costume and action of Copley's Mars—both equally typical of the French stage—compare Pietro Martini's plate for *Issipile,* Act II, Scene XII, in Vol. II, of *Le Opere di Pietro Metastasio,* Paris, 1780–82 (Fig. 106). From some other bookplate Copley no doubt also copied a *Battle Scene* (pen drawing of 1754, in the Addison Gallery at Andover, Mass.).

[3]*Copley-Pelham Letters, loc. cit.,* July 11, 1774.

it was published in 1775. A few other English painters who were then in Rome all but ignored the eclectic trend, namely, Joseph Wright of Derby and George Romney. Perhaps the only British artists who were still hopelessly sold on eclecticism were Gavin Hamilton, who lived permanently in Rome, and Henri Fuseli, who lived there for a long time.

Younger artists were holding the stage when Copley came; men of stronger, more genuine talents. Young Jacques Louis David came at the same time as a student to the French Academy. Young Francisco Goya was there until the summer of 1775. Even one made less immune than Copley by twenty years of colonial portraiture against eclectic classicism was not likely to catch the disease as badly as West did.

Only in one field did the Roman influence have a devastating effect on Copley. That field was religious painting. It almost made another Benjamin West out of him; witness, his diploma picture, *The Tribute Money.* It hangs close enough to West's *Christ blessing little Children* in the Diploma Gallery of the Royal Academy at London to prove to any one that I am not exaggerating.

On the other hand, Copley's continental tour gave him a broader knowledge of the European art which so far he had known only from hearsay. Before he went to Rome he saw Paris, and on his way back to London he visited Florence, Parma, Mantua, Venice, Amsterdam, Brussels, and Antwerp. When at last he arrived in London, he came with the experience of a connoisseur. He did not come as a beginner who sought instruction. This was important for his future career—considering the ramified metropolitan school which comprised literally hundreds of painters.

Every one of these Englishmen was probably more interesting to Copley than was the American, Benjamin West, who, generous and helpful as he was, invited Copley to stay at his home. Copley was West's friend only on the surface and only for a short while. After ten years Copley's hostility to that only other American member of the Royal Academy was no longer a secret. At the meetings of the Academicians Copley opposed West's moves. In 1803 the rift between the two burst wide open. In that year West sent his painting *Hagar and Ishmael* to the exhibition, though it had been shown before, and that was a violation of the rules. Copley, who painted the same subject in 1798, naturally remembered the first showing and took this opportunity to expose the President as an impostor—probably to undermine his position, which was none too good anyway. In the following year Copley voted against the re-election of West.

## II. *British Painters in Copley's London*

Who were the British artists with whom Copley associated? To enumerate all of them would be tantamount to reprinting the roster of the Royal Academicians from 1779 to 1815.

But to gain some perspective on the painters who were active in London during the forty years in which, as Dunlap said, "Copley ceased to be an American painter in feeling," it is advisable to consider the several generational groups separately; namely, those who were older than Copley, those who were his own age, and those who were younger. For what we are wont to call a period of art is not the unit it is supposed to be. The artistic mentality of a period, its temper, its problems and its inspirations, spring from the incessant struggle between the widely different opinions of artists old, middle-aged, and young. The older men are generally looked upon by all their juniors as old-fashioned and the young are generally looked upon by all their seniors as rebels. It is that struggle between the generations which causes art to develop. The development of British art from 1775 to 1815, of which Copley was a part, was no exception to the rule. It was determined by the polarity of men of different age who lived and worked together in London, the one pulling backward, the other pulling forward, and yet others who steered a middle course.

Octogenarians and septuagenarians, such as Thomas Hudson and Joseph Highmore, whose influence was felt in the colonies when

Copley was still there, now lived in retirement: Hudson among his collections of old masters at Twickenham; Highmore at Canterbury. Richard Wilson, the landscape painter, was too old and his field of interest was too remote to impress a thirty-eight-year-old portraitist and still-life painter of colonial extraction. Moreover, none of these veterans lived longer than the middle of the 'eighties.

The two most important painters of the next younger generation died before 1800, namely, Sir Joshua Reynolds, who was fifty-two at Copley's coming, and Thomas Gainsborough, who was forty-eight. No sign of influence is noticeable between Copley and George Stubbs, the famous anatomist of the horse and the President of the Society of British Artists, where Copley's pictures were exhibited beginning with the year 1766.

Artists of Copley's age, that is, in their thirties, of course exercised the strongest influence upon his development. Among these there were portrait and conversation-piece painters. Two of them had been in Rome and had returned to London at the same time as Copley: George Romney and Joseph Wright of Derby.

Throughout his life Wright's and Copley's names were coupled as by a curious whim of destiny. Both became known in London in the same year and at the same exhibition. In 1766, Wright's *Orrery* and Copley's *Boy with the Squirrel* hung side by side at the show of the Incorporated Society of Artists, and from that day the British public could never tell the two painters apart. Wright's manner resembled Copley's—probably because both descended more or less directly from Hudson. I doubt, however, that the two painters saw much of each other personally. Wright did not live in London, but at Bath. John Zoffani, the legitimate successor to Hogarth as the master of the conversation piece, was also of Copley's age. But Zoffani was too long absent from London to count him as a possible influence; long journeys to Florence, Vienna, and India removed him often for decades from the London scene.

Two history painters deserve special attention, the Alsatian Philip James de Loutherbourg and the Irishman James Barry.

Before more research has been done, I cannot give more than my personal opinion on the probable relations between Copley and de Loutherbourg. The latter was three years younger than Copley. In my mind there is no doubt that his battle pieces owed their dramatic mood and sometimes even their compositions to Copley's. The connection between the two artists has never been seriously considered, but it should be. Copley's works antedated those of de Loutherbourg which remind me of them. For example, *The Defeat of the Floating Batteries at Gibraltar* was completed a dozen or so years before Lord Fornbough presented de Loutherbourg's *Defeat of the Spanish Armada* to Greenwich Hospital.

James Barry, four years younger than Copley, was back from Rome when Copley came to London. As an Academician and a renowned history painter, Barry was worth courting. But our excessively well-groomed and mannered little Bostonian was probably as little anxious as any one of his British colleagues to run into that arrogant and quarrelsome Irishman whose "dirty appearance" and "savage deportment" were notorious; eventually he was thrown out of the Royal Academy because it was impossible to get along with him. Nevertheless, Copley, as a devotee to historical painting, seems to have profited from Barry's murals, *The Development of Civilization,* which decorate the Great Room of the Royal Society of Arts. Their manner was grand, and, in a sense, revolutionized the style of history painting. When they were still being painted, Copley was grappling with his first great historical canvas, *The Death of the Earl of Chatham,* and before their completion, which took Barry six years, the murals were twice exhibited to the public.

Immediately following the second exhibit, some one suggested to the Government of the United States that a London painter be invited to America to paint a series of pictures of the life of George Washington. Henry Laurens of South Carolina, then in London to sign the preliminaries of the treaty of peace, was officially delegated to select an artist of merit and it was said that he "viewed all the great painters in London" before he decided on James Barry. This assurance will not be taken too seriously by those who are privy to the ways in which selections and awards are wont to be handled. Then, as today, it was more convenient for a delegate first to consult one of his friends who was an expert, and, if the friend had any advice, to accept it gladly and act upon it. Whom else should Henry Laurens have consulted but Copley? For Copley, just then, was painting the *Portrait of Henry Laurens* (1782). The portrait was burned in 1861 and is known only from engravings. The interesting fact that no one recommended Benjamin West likewise suggests that Copley was pulling the wires. William T. Whitley wonders why Copley was not himself suggested for the job, for "Copley's talents were exactly suitable."[4] This, I am afraid, none but a prophet could have foretold in 1782 when *The Death of the Earl of Chatham* was all that Copley could show up as proof of his talent as a history painter. Besides, what the Americans wanted was a *series* of murals. Copley had never tried his hand on a series and was probably not over-anxious to attempt one since *The Death of the Earl of Chatham* had taken him years to finish. On the other hand, it is quite possible that he really admired Barry's series and honestly proposed his name to Mr. Laurens. Barry turned the invitation down. One cannot help thinking, had Copley suggested himself and been chosen—what then? Not only would Copley have disengaged himself from the influence of British art before it smothered him; not only would he have gained new strength from the renewed contact with his native environment; but the whole future of painting in America would have become different. It was a critical moment. But the opportunity was missed.

## III. *Copley's British Portraiture*

I do not intend to discuss every picture that Copley painted in England. Many of them are of no interest in a history of American

[4]W. T. Whitley, *Artists and Their Friends in England, op. cit.*, I, p. 375.

art. His single portraits and conversation pieces formed a continuation of what he had done in New England. But they did not progress in the direction of his New England development. The style of his London portraits was the result of a compromise with the fashionable British manner.

Evidently, the painter's concern was no longer with characterization but with elegant appearance. The change in Copley's approach from rustic directness to metropolitan elegance is apparent if the full-length of *Colonel Jeremiah Lee* (1769, Boston Museum of Fine Arts, Fig. 107) is compared with the full-length of *Brass Crosby, the Lord Mayor of London* (1780–90, Chicago Art Institute, Fig. 108). From his Anglified point of view Copley probably frowned on his colonial efforts as a cavalier *à la mode* frowns on a boor. All that mattered to him was the technical progress he had made since he left Boston. He had followed the advice of Joshua Reynolds: he had availed himself of the advantages of the example which he could have in Europe. As a result, he had broken away from what the metropolitans sarcastically had called "his own little way in Boston." He had learned to use the British clair-obscure method with which one can subordinate a multiplicity of objects to a few dominant accents; with which one can harmonize all colors, instead of isolating the local colors; and with which one can immerse an entire figure in the atmosphere of its setting. What Copley did not notice, or perhaps did not care to notice, was that in the process of his transformation the natural simplicity of direct statements which marked his colonial style became supplanted by an artificial simplification, a more or less arbitrary application of a technical method.

The saddest thing is that, try as he would, Copley never approximated the British method of simplification—as the comparison of any Copley of this period with any Gainsborough or even any Hoppner will reveal. The reason for his shortcoming was that Copley remained in London the "still-life painter" that he had been in Boston. But while he used to control his still-life and treat of it with great economy in Boston, where his objective was concentrated characterization, now, in Europe, where the organization of a portrait was directed by another compositional method, Copley lost all regard for what was essential and what was negligible.

It is interesting that an undue prominence of accessories became noticeable for the first time in the Roman portrait of *Mr. and Mrs. Ralph Izard,* of 1775, admittedly his first serious essay in "composition" (Fig. 109). There is a Greek amphora upon a parapet, a cast of the Orestes-Electra group on the Louis-Seize table, a drawing after that group in Mr. Izard's hand, the drape, and the Roman Colosseum seen through enframing pillars. The *Copley-Clarke Family Picture* (*circa* 1780, privately owned in Washington, D. C.), which he painted about five years later, is a veritable storehouse of decorative still-life.[5] A sofa is seen against the vista of a park. There are drapes and columns, scrolls, a child's rattle, a hat and feathers, elaborate periwigs and robes. These overstressed appurtenances distinguish Copley's ambitious conversation piece of six life-sized figures from those conversation pieces in the genuine British tradition which Copley tried to emulate, *e.g., The Locker Family Picture,* by John Francis Rigaut (1779, London, Arthur De Casseres).[6] Yet, the *Copley Family Picture* seems an unobtrusive arrangement if it is compared with *The Royal Princesses* (1785, Buckingham Palace, Fig. 110) of another five years later. In this large conversation piece, motifs from Reynolds' *The Graces Decorating Hymen* (London, National Gallery) were crowded into a perfect bedlam of still-life. In a caustic criticism of this picture, which appeared in *The Morning Post* of May 5, 1785, John Hoppner expressed the British point of view, but also, in a sense, the whole tragedy of Copley: "Is it, Mr. Copley, because you have heard that fine feathers make fine birds that you have concluded that fine clothes will make fine princesses? What delightful disorder! Why, you have plucked up harmony by the roots and planted confusion in its stead! Princesses, parrots, dogs, grapes, flowers, leaves are each

[5]B. N. Parker and A. B. Wheeler, *loc. cit.,* Plate 130.
[6]Sacheverell Sitwell, *Conversation Pieces,* London, 1937, Plate 104.

striving for pre-eminence and opposing with hostile force all attempts of our wearied eyes to find repose."

## IV. *Copley's Historical Pictures*

The student of American art, as I just said, need not waste any time on Copley's vagaries in portrait painting. What really matters when we study Copley in Europe is his history pictures. These were the first great contributions of an American artist to the art of Europe. The trend of history painting which was inaugurated by the "still-life painter" Copley differed fundamentally from the idealistic methods of the eclectic school of Benjamin West. Let it be said emphatically: John Singleton Copley, not Benjamin West, occasioned the revolution of history painting. Unmindful of historical data, art lovers of today may have little praise for Copley's *Death of the Earl of Chatham* or its several successors, and the historian may find much fault with the individual specimens of Copley's painted history. But there is no denying that the evolution of realistic history painting, in France from Baron Gros to Delaroche and Meissonier, and in Germany from Wilhelm Kaulbach to Karl Piloty and Adolf Menzel, originated from the work of John Singleton Copley of Boston. He was the first to envisage historical painting in the still-life way, in other words, as events of history recorded in regard to settings, faces, and costumes faithfully down to the minutiæ of field glasses, boots, and buttons. Trumbull, too, who painted the first historical murals in the United States, stemmed from Copley. As has been shown, Copley's conversation pieces were amplified still-lives. As will be shown, Copley's history pictures were amplified conversation pieces. Some hundred and fifty years before Copley, Velasquez went the same way from still-life to group portraits and from group portraits to histories. His *Surrender of Breda* was really a great group portrait. In the eighteenth century the work of the great Spanish realist had been obliterated by the eclectic classicists of Italy, France, and England. Now an American made another bold start. The influence of England may have made

Copley's task difficult. But it was only in England that he could solve it successfully, and London offered a better platform than Boston from which to be heard everywhere in Europe. But what was heard in Europe did not originate from European traditions. It originated from the core of the American tradition.

When Copley went to London he did not just exchange the colonial method of expression for the British method of expression. The "still-life approach," deeply rooted in the colonial tradition of the character portrait, was ingrained in Copley, and so it persisted even after he had acquired British habits. Besides, the colonial and the British manners were unassimilable. The "still-life approach" could not be absorbed by the "compositional approach" any more than the inductive method of thinking could be absorbed by the deductive method of thinking. This is no far-fetched figure of speech. When Copley painted the portrait of *Mrs. Thomas Boylston* of Boston, his procedure was "inductive." He worked out from separate given facts and built other given facts around them until the artist's "generalization" of the old lady's personality was formulated on the canvas. Benjamin West's approach, on the other hand, was "deductive." When West painted *The Death of Wolfe,* he worked out from a compositional formula and made the separate facts (if such they were) subservient to it. William Hazlitt was alluding to West's deductive facility when he declared "West has no good quality save composition."[7] The incompatibility of the two manners was the ultimate reason why Copley "murdered the king's English" in such portraits as *The Royal Princesses.* But when it came to history pictures, he was in even greater danger.

Copley's portraiture had a solid foundation. Even those painted under British influence issued from the tradition of the earlier colonial portraits from the limners to Robert Feke. But for his history pictures he could find no point of departure in American art. His only possible point of departure was the British tradition of history painting. British history painting, however, depended first

[7]W. T. Whitley, *Art in England, 1800–1820, op. cit.,* p. 225.

and last on "composition" and offered little, if any, opening for the colonial "still-life approach." The conflict becomes apparent in Copley's first ambitious venture, *The Death of the Earl of Chatham* (Fig. 6).[8]

It was without precedent that an event of contemporary history, which happened only a year before the painting was begun, was chosen for the theme of a monumental painting. This was not, as West's *Death of Wolfe* or *William Penn's Treaty with the Indians,* history removed from the realness of the day by romantic notions of distant Canada or Pennsylvania or of picturesque Indians and Indian rituals. This was London in 1778. This was the elder William Pitt; this was the apoplectic fit he suffered in the presence of the House of Lords after his speech against the severance of the colonies from the Crown. The fifty-five persons were portrayed from life. Every spectator knew the originals. No more "modern" departure from the conventional standards of history painting could be imagined.[9]

Still, as regards the form of the whole, Copley started out from a compositional pattern, as every other British history painter used to do. His first sketch (British Museum, Fig. 111) reminds one in a general way of Raphael; at any rate it would have done nicely for

[8]His very first experiment, *Brook Watson saved from a Shark in Savannah Harbour,* already showed the important features that were henceforth to distinguish Copley's manner of narrative from West's. A story about a well-known, living person was told in terms of portraits. But the trivial episode from the youth of the Commissioner General of the British army in America classes the picture with genre painting, at any rate, outside the domain of history painting. The original painting is owned by Lord Aberdere in London. Replicas are in the Foundling Hospital in London and in the Art Museum of Boston. Frank Bayley (*The Life and Works of John S. Copley,* Boston, 1915) states that the original sketch for the whole is in the possession of Mrs. F. Gordon Dexter of Boston.

[9]The painting was produced in three years of tremendous effort (1779–81), in competition with sculptor John Bacon and painter Nicholas Read. The competition was sponsored by the Corporation of London. The original canvas hung until recently in the House of Parliament at London. It was exhibited at the Metropolitan Museum in New York early in 1937.

any idealistic painting in the accepted classical manner. There is a semicircular surround; below it a central pyramid, comprising the dying hero and his anxious friends, is enframed by two symmetrical pillar-like groups of figures on either side. The sketch provided for seven dominant figures, about as many lesser figures, and yet as many subordinate figures. The composition assured a perfect pictorial unity for the twenty-one figures. But it was warped until it broke to pieces when "still-life painter" Copley filled it up with fifty-five figures and began to consider all the factual circumstances of the historic event. He wished to make clear that there had been the two opposing parties—and so his composition split into two: the Minority around Lord Mansfield on the left and the Majority around the stricken Earl of Chatham on the right. An experienced British history painter would have seen no dilemma. He would have treated Mansfield and Chatham as equal pictorial values; he would have made each person the core of a group and would have made the two groups correspond visually. But Copley's conscientious abiding by the known facts did not admit of such a solution. It was on record that, while every one else in the house rose to his feet when Chatham collapsed, Lord Mansfield alone remained seated. This had to be stated in the picture. Again, an experienced British painter would have ignored the record for the sake of the picture. If Mansfield was to be seen, and all others were standing, he had to stand too. In Copley's picture the seated figure of Lord Mansfield, far off in the left distance, was completely lost amidst all the tall men standing in front of him. It seems that Lord Mansfield himself thought this was adding insult to injury. It was bad enough that his enemy, the Earl of Chatham, was so glorified; it was an outrage to reduce Lord Mansfield to such inconspicuousness. At all events, his Lordship refused to pose for Copley until two years after the picture had been publicly shown. The vigorous full-length portrait of *Lord Mansfield* (London, National Portrait Gallery, Fig. 114) was based on the *sketch* that was made for the *Death of*

*Chatham* (Fig. 113), but was not executed until 1783, when at last Copley was granted permission to paint the head from life.

In every instance, the numerous sketches which Copley drew in preparation for his canvas were simpler than the respective sections in the finished painting. Each of them would have been a strong vehicle for a few figures. But the "still-life painter" began to stuff each of these compositional units with more and more figures until the same thing happened to them that happened to the sketch of the whole; the constructive form was stretched until it burst asunder. Compare the group around the dying Earl of Chatham as it was treated in the painting (Fig. 6) and as it was treated in the sketch (Fig. 112). In the painting it became overcrowded and had to be too far-spread; in the sketch, with only five figures, everything was convincing and lucid.

The last-named *charcoal drawing* may at the same time demonstrate Copley's troubles in another direction. It shows that the conflict between the British and colonial traditions was not confined to the problems of form and composition, but also to the conception of the subject matter. It will be noticed from the drawing that Copley at first thought of representing the Peers in their street clothes. This would have been correct. No member of the House of Lords wore his scarlet-and-gold regalia on the occasion of a parliamentary debate. Copley's departure from facts, about which he must have been informed, can be explained only by the fear on his part of carrying his inroads into academic dogmas too far. Heaven knows how often Sir Joshua Reynolds warned the painters that "common nature" was incompatible with the heroic style. So Copley lent a more pompous note to his scene by draping the Peers in costumes which must have been painful for any Englishman to behold. The public resented this breach of etiquette as much as the untruthfulness of the setting. I have no explanation to offer for the fact that Copley admittedly never took a look at the inside of the House of Lords, but relied wholly on his imagination. To what extent Copley departed from "common nature" and tried to view his story from an heroic angle is best illustrated by his calling the picture *The Death* of Chatham. It was common knowledge that William Pitt died a month after his speech, and that he died not in Parliament but at his country estate in Kent. It also was common knowledge that Chatham's collapse after his famous address had nothing at all to do with the content of the speech or the emotions it aroused. The newspapers mentioned the fact that Pitt's fainting spell was caused by poor ventilation in the House of Lords.[10]

Copley's next historical canvas showed the "still-life approach" getting the better of the "compositional approach." Perhaps the compositional manner would have become obliterated even more in factual reporting had Copley next tried his hand on another historical subject in the relatively quiet vein of *The Death of Chatham* instead of venturing forth to more complicated performances. But he was too ambitious to repeat himself. Instead of giving himself time to solve simpler tasks in a more satisfactory manner, he pressed on toward more dramatic themes which involved more action, a more excited illumination, and were altogether too difficult for him, at least for the time being.

Three years after the completion of *The Death of Chatham* he attempted a battle picture, *The Death of Major Peirson* (1784, London, Tate Gallery, Fig. 7). Since we know that battle pictures were not uncommon in London before West's *Death of Wolfe,* and since we further know that Copley was no follower of West, let us not perpetuate an error made by all the earlier historians, namely, that Copley's picture was inspired by West. The stilted and colorless *Death of Wolfe* pales into insignificance beside the dynamic action and sparkling brushwork of Copley's painting. Every one must have felt this at the time when the painting was exhibited in Alderman Boydell's Gallery with Copley's portrait, painted by Gilbert Stuart, included in the frame. (The portrait is now in the National Portrait Gallery at London.)

[10]W. T. Whitley, *Artists and Their Friends in England, op. cit.,* I, p. 362.

Again the event represented was of recent date. It was an episode of the battle of St. Heliers, Jersey, which occurred in 1781. Again all the main figures were portraits of living persons. Ensigns Rowan and Smith were bearing the flags. Lieutenant Drysdale was carrying the body of Major Peirson out of the battle. Lieutenant Buchanan was supporting the fallen Major's knees. Looking down into the young commander's face were Adjutant Harrison and Captain Corbett. Captain Hemerey was seen rushing in from the right. The fleeing civilians on the right were Mrs. Copley, the nurse with the baby, and John Singleton Copley, Junior, who was later Baron Lyndhurst.

An innovation of great significance was the unity of bright cool light, the luminous atmosphere of an early January morning, in which both the setting and the actors were immersed. This time, the large phrases and lines of the original sketch were not nearly as badly destroyed when Copley spelled out details on the canvas which were only implied in the sketch.[11] Nor did the artist this time depart from "common nature" in obeisance to the false pretenses of the heroic style. The canvas is alive with direct studies from life and each of them betrays the genius of the "still-life painter." Even modern eyes are fascinated by the forceful coloration of the scarlet uniforms, the yellow flag and the blue, white, and red flag. A perfect gem of a color study is Major Peirson's colored servant. His black skin and his dark-blue jacket stand out beautifully between the scarlet-and-gold uniforms of the enframing officers. But the prize

[11]Nevertheless, the sketch of the whole (owned at one time by Messrs. Leggatt, London) was simpler and more unified than the painting. In the painting most of the original motifs were doubled. Only one flag, instead of two, was planned for the center. The fighters rose in a more coherent cadence from the left toward the flag; their mass was less split up into separate combatants. Only two men attended the dying French officer in the right-hand middle distance, where the painting gives numerous soldiers about a cannon. The group of fugitives on the extreme right was originally planned as a solid mass, not as two separate units; the fleeing boy was seen in front of his mother, not at her side.—A collection of preparatory drawings, owned by Lord Aberdere, shows in detail how Copley was sidetracked toward a more refractionated painting.

goes to the colored man's three-cornered hat, magnificent with sky-blue, gray, and black plumes and magnificently viewed against a cloud of white powder smoke.

Another year after this Copley came forth with a much more complicated battle picture, a battle at sea, the most ambitious thing he ever attempted. This was *The Defeat of the Floating Batteries at Gibraltar* under Sir George Elliot, who was later Lord Heathfield (1783–91, London, Guild Hall). He spent six years of work on it. When it was shown for the first time, the success was enormous; in fact, it occasioned for the next ten years a minor flood of marine battle pictures in London.

In this one instance Copley derived some inspiration from West's *Battle of La Hogue,* in which similar episodes were displayed: a towering ship, ablaze on the left, pours forth an arch of fire and smoke toward the right. This forms the background for boats tossed about with men falling overboard or clambering back.[12] Copley was extremely careful this time that every detail in his painting should correspond exactly with the historical event and setting. In 1786 a visitor found the painter in his studio "literally laying siege to Gibraltar, as he has his models arranged before him in all stages of progress, not only for the fortress, but of gunboats, ship-tackle, men, and every instrument of destruction."[13] In the following year Copley made a special trip to Hanover to paint from life the German officers who had participated in the battle.

But in the end it was the old story over again. The task was too difficult for any "still-life painter." The important motif of flaming ships floating on the waves entailed effects of a colorful chiaroscuro which were beyond his power. Moreover, Copley became lost in the maze of interminable details. Some of the preparatory studies were excellently composed (Fig. 116), but lost their significance in

[12]The date of John Trumbull's *Sortie from Gibraltar* (1789) precludes the possibility that Copley received his inspiration from there. Rather is it true that Copley's composition inspired Trumbull.

[13]W. T. Whitley, *Artists and Their Friends in England, op. cit.,* II, p. 137.

the overcrowded painting. The canvas was too large for his studio. Standing on a platform which could be raised or lowered to give him a few square feet to work upon, Copley painted detail for detail without a chance of viewing the whole from a distance. When the picture was finished it was, at best, an aggregate of fine heads, figures and episodes.[14]

It is significant that the best and the most lasting value that came from the six years of labor which Copley spent on his canvas was a little by-product, the *Oil Sketch of Lord Heathfield* (1787, London, National Portrait Gallery, Fig. 8). The portrait was probably done in less than an hour. But that short space of time was one of Copley's happiest moments of inspiration. The *Heathfield* is a bit of sterling *painting*. It shows what Copley could do when he set every other consideration aside and abandoned himself, as in bygone colonial days, whole-heartedly to the "painting business." *The Defeat of the Floating Batteries* attracts the attention of a very few, but whoever visits the National Portrait Gallery stops before the little portrait of *Lord Heathfield,* as he does before the full-length of *Lord Mansfield* (Fig. 114), which hangs near by.

Copley's idea of expanding the conversation piece into a new type of realistic history picture did not have much of a following in the British School. It bore fruit in America and France, but not in England, except for the history pictures of the Preraphaelites which were indirectly linked with Copley's initiative via the Parisian and Antwerp schools of the early nineteenth century.

Much more attention was given in England to Copley's methods of exploiting art commercially, above all to his tent shows. I have mentioned the fact that Copley used to show his history paintings separately in "pavilions" at an enormous profit. His invention was imitated by West who filled the coffers of the Pennsylvania Hospital with the returns of the separate exhibitions of *Christ Healing the*

[14] Preparatory charcoal drawings are in the Print Room of the British Museum. A small monochrome of the whole is in the London Foundling Hospital (Fig. 115). The canvas in Guild Hall is very badly damaged.

*Sick.* Rembrandt Peale eventually made $9000 in a single year from touring the United States with his *Court of Death.* Samuel F. B. Morse, who was less lucky, showed his *House of Representatives* in an itinerant tent show. The idea was kept alive by the panoramas of battles and landscapes. With these Copley was also connected. Henry Aston Barker's panoramas of *The Fleet at Spithead, The Battle of the Nile,* and *The Battle of Copenhagen* were probably inspired by Copley's pavilion exhibition of *The Defeat of the Floating Batteries.* In this context it is well to remember that the ancestral type of the real panorama—the *Eidophusicon,* an invention of Philip de Loutherbourg—was first displayed in the year in which Copley startled London with the pavilion exhibition of *The Death of Chatham.*[15]

Copley's later historical paintings do not warrant a fuller discussion. What we learn from them is that even Copley, once the soundest empiricist of his period, was lured away to historical subjects of a dead past—due to the rising tide of romantic historicism.

*Charles I, demanding the Five Impeached Members of Parliament* (1799, Boston Public Library, Fig. 117) was laboriously patched together from all kinds of historic "references." The interior of the original House of Commons was reconstructed from "curious and authentic drawings" which a member of the Society of Antiquarians had furnished. Every historical character was likewise reconstructed from engravings, medals and busts of artists of the Stuart period. A separate list of the authorities that had been consulted for authentic heads was published.[16] It included the names of Sir Anthony van Dyck, Peter Lely, Samuel Cooper, and William Dobson as well as numerous other old painters, Dutch, Italian, and French. No one who knows in what measure Copley was dependent on the fullness of life will be surprised that the painting he pro-

[15]W. T. Whitley, *Artists and Their Friends in England, op. cit.,* I, p. 353, and II, pp. 352 ff.

[16]The reference list was appended to the prospectus by which a forthcoming engraving after the painting was advertised to potential subscribers.

duced under these circumstances was a conglomeration of lifeless heads attached to bodies that gesticulated like puppets. The *Offer of the Crown to Lady Jane Grey* (1808, Boston, Mrs. Gordon Dexter), was, as Frank Bayley said, "large and important," but that is the most that can be said of it.

Manifestly these late pictures were no longer "American in feeling." The empiricist Copley, who used to tax the patience of his colonial sitters when he matched every tint on the canvas with the actual color of things before him, was at this time brooding like an alchemist over chimerical secrets of "color harmony" which were said to have been lost. That was one of the symptoms of an age that had forfeited every bit of naïveté and directness. West was advocating the "rainbow theory," Copley was concocting the "Venetian vehicle."

In 1797 a certain Captain Morely discovered what he said was the secret of Titian's coloring. His "Venetian Secret" was communicated to Benjamin West and was afterwards peddled to at least seven different academicians, each of whom paid ten guineas for it.[17] Copley was left out and became so intrigued by the whole thing that he locked himself up and made experiments of his own until he invented what he called the "Venetian vehicle." In 1802 his son wrote to his sister in Boston: "Henceforth you may fairly expect that our father's pictures will transcend the productions even of Titian himself." Apparently he was fully in earnest.

From whatever angle Copley's latest products are approached, nobody, I believe, would contradict what Samuel Morse wrote in 1811 in his *Letters and Journals:* "Copley's power of mind has almost entirely left him. His last paintings are miserable."

The saddest part of it was that Copley himself realized that he was a failure. In 1800 an interviewer for *The British Magazine* described him as "a prey to chagrin and disappointment." It was hard to admit defeat if one had as ambitious a head as Copley.

[17]W. T. Whitley, *Artists and Their Friends in England, op. cit.,* II, pp. 209–212, relates the absurd story at length.

The personal tragedy of Copley was the general tragedy of colonial culture on a smaller scale. In all cultural matters the influence of England grew overwhelmingly great toward the end of the eighteenth century. The farther the colonies withdrew politically from the mother country the more the colonial gentry aped the British taste and scoffed at their fathers' "own little ways." Colonial architects imitated Gibbs and Sir William Chambers. Colonial poets, as David Humphreys said, "strove to approach the perfection of Pope and the sweetness of his versification." In painting Copley strove for something similar when he, who had loved to observe and recreate knotty characters, set out in quest of Titian's coloration.

At the time of the Declaration of Independence Copley's art was the consummation of American independent art. When he submitted to the demands of European art, which was in its dotage, he foreswore the independent American tradition. As to who was victor in the struggle between West and Copley the judges left no doubt. West was interred in the Cathedral of St. Paul, Copley in the parish churchyard of Croydon.

# *CONCLUSION*

FROM the beginning of art in America, in the seventeenth century, throughout its development in the eighteenth century, one thing has been constantly in evidence: the conflict between the colonial and European traditions which earlier in this volume I compared to the current and the countercurrent in the evolutionary stream. This conflict was not as sharp in the early colonial period with Smibert and Feke as it was in the middle colonial period with West and Copley. In the late colonial period the British manner of Gilbert Stuart ruled in America over all rivals.

The colonial tradition was perpetuated only by a few native painters who stayed in their country through the Revolutionary War, Charles Wilson Peale, Ralph Earl, and John Trumbull. Peale came to Boston in 1775 and filled the place that Copley had vacated the year before. He was Copley's logical successor. And so was Trumbull, whose portrait of *The Family of Jonathan Trumbull* (1777, Yale University Art Gallery, Fig. 118) evinces the Spartan sobriety, the cool crisp coloration, and the explicit design that distinguished the colonial from the British work of Copley. Indeed, its angular construction is reminiscent of Robert Feke's *Royall Family Picture.* Ralph Earl was likewise "the careful, interested painter of things as they were, and no matter how quibbling his touch . . ., how naïve his execution, we are made to feel that his performance was gained from a straightforward and honest manner of approach."[1]

But the endeavors of these loyal colonials to continue in the tradition of Feke and Copley was considered old-fashioned and outmoded after 1793. In that year Gilbert Stuart returned to the United States after an absence of eighteen years in England and

[1]Daniel Catton Rich, *International Studio* (May–August, 1930), pp. 36 ff.

Ireland. He returned as a practitioner of every accepted British standard of good taste. Such a virtuoso of the brush had not been known in America. Let it be remembered that the decisive change from the middle colonial to the English metropolitan manner had so far occurred only in England; the people of America were unaware of West's and Copley's British work. Stuart's paintings were the first examples of that fashionable manner in the New World. We are prone to forget, moreover, that Stuart's likenesses, above all those of George Washington, were not at all American in conception and execution. The regal majesty, the splendor of the lighting and of the coloration, classed the Washington full-lengths with the conventional portraits of French and English royalty. It is a fallacy to rate Gilbert Stuart as a sterling American painter because he painted so many sterling Americans. Painting native Americans does not automatically place the painter in the American tradition.

Unfortunately it has become the fashion to evaluate colonial painting by critical standards that are derived from European art and, worse yet, to evaluate it by the external measure of technical proficiency. As a result, the painters of the Revolution, Ralph Earl in particular, have been sadly misjudged. Earl was not a sorcerer like Stuart. But that is no reason to classify Earl or any other colonial painter as a mediocrity. To do so is fundamentally uncritical; it confuses the whole issue.

Shall we regard it as axiomatic that the only painter worth remembering is one who has acquired a nice manual deftness from a high-class academic teacher? Shall we dismiss as inconsequential the artist who was inexperienced in the use of studio tricks and perhaps for that very reason all the more independent? To illustrate my point: The paintings of Ralph Earl convey the New England atmosphere of their day as appreciably as Copley's colonial paintings did. At any rate, they convey more of that impalpable colonial aura than all of Stuart's skillfully painted performances put together. Earl was a cumbersome designer and a quaint narrator of details. He did not possess Stuart's knack of overlooking the details for the benefit of a more dashing ensemble effect. But every hard detail and every rigid line he drew *characterized* the particular people who sat for him. Stuart's dabs of the brush and nuances of the palette may have been more tricky and the atmospheric transitions of his clair-obscure more sublime, but the cleverness of his manipulation did not make him superior to the humble painters who noted values that he neglected. The humble painters did not slight anything. They saw things and persons penetratingly. Peale's portraits were drier and Trumbull's were colder than Stuart's. But the Spartan spirit of the portraits of Peale and Trumbull were intensely characteristic of the mind and the temper of Revolutionary America. Stuart's British-trained eyes, naturally, never noticed such things.

Ralph Earl was the American counterpart of the Englishman Stuart in another sense also. Stuart ran away from America, Earl ran away from England. Stuart ran away from America on the last boat that escaped British detention the day before Bunker Hill and would probably never have returned had not his debts compelled him to run away from his creditors in Dublin. When Stuart returned to America he brought everything English with him. When Earl left England he left everything English behind. Earl had been a student of Sir Joshua Reynolds during his sojourn in England (1779–87), but upon his return to America he dismissed the methods and manners the head of the British school had imparted to him. Late portraits of Ralph Earl, such as the *Colonel Benjamin Tallmadge,* or the *Mrs. Benjamin Tallmadge and Her Children* (1792, Historical Society, Litchfield, Conn., Fig. 119) resemble the likenesses of the early colonial limners. The resemblance is grounded in the fact that the style of the limners and the style of Earl were both unlike anything European. In other words, both were uniquely independent. The limners were independent out of ignorance of other countries' manners. Earl was consciously independent. He repudiated the manner he had been taught in England.

The example of Earl should warn us that there is something better than manual brilliance, namely, the direct and instinctive response to what is profoundly *felt* and inclusively perceived. No matter how "primitive" the means by which the feeling and the perception are expressed, the expression is more telling than the most brilliant performance which lacks a message.

The colonial tradition had no use for virtuosity. That was as it should be. The colonies were a primitive country and virtuosity belongs with hypercivilization. Virtuosity is a symptom of art in an aged civilization. It always crops up at the end of an evolution; never in its formative phase. When all other means of expression have been exhausted, when artists have nothing else to communicate and the public nothing else to get excited over, then surface graces and clever effects are their last resort.

Without the strength that came from youth the dominance of European mannerisms would not have been overthrown as it was after the death of Gilbert Stuart. But other European mannerisms kept flowing into American studios. The struggle between the two opposite trends did not stop. Time and again the stream of history was churned by the fighting crosscurrents. Every rising generation in America, as I have pointed out, had among its artists leaders who stood for Europe and leaders who stood for America. We have seen the polarity of John Smibert and Robert Feke, of West and Copley, of Stuart and Earl. As I said in the second chapter of this book, the phenomenon recurred in Thomas Cole and Asher Brown Durand; in James McNeill Whistler and Winslow Homer.

These later generations fall outside the scope of this book. Nevertheless, if a glance is cast ahead, not only will the tenor of what has been said be clarified, but something will become apparent which has not yet been said, but should be said in conclusion. What this forward glance would show is the gradual penetration of the American tradition into the consciousness of the American artists.

Throughout the eighteenth century the polarity of American and European art was hardly felt. To follow the one or the other tradition was a matter of instinct, not of principle. None of the artists of whom we have spoken was aware of the consequences that his allegiance to either the British or the American way might have on the future of American art. None felt responsible for that future. In the nineteenth century, however, the followers of the American way became increasingly aware of their responsibility.

From the beginning it was a fact of history that the future greatness of American art depended on the growth of an indigenous tradition. But the fact remained hidden until late and the truth that followed from it was not enunciated until Thomas Eakins, in 1914, spoke to the American press: "If America is to produce great painters and if young art students wish to assume a place in the history of the art of their country, their first desire should be to remain in America, to peer deeper into the heart of American life, rather than to spend their time abroad obtaining a superficial view of the art of the Old World. . . . They must strike out for themselves, and only by doing this will we create a great and distinctly American art."[2]

[2]Quoted from Lloyd Goodrich, *Thomas Eakins; His Life and Work,* New York, 1933, p. 139.

2

JOHN SMIBERT: ALLAN RAMSAY. ENGRAVING BY VERCRUYSSE

3

JOHN SMIBERT: DEAN BERKELEY AND HIS ENTOURAGE

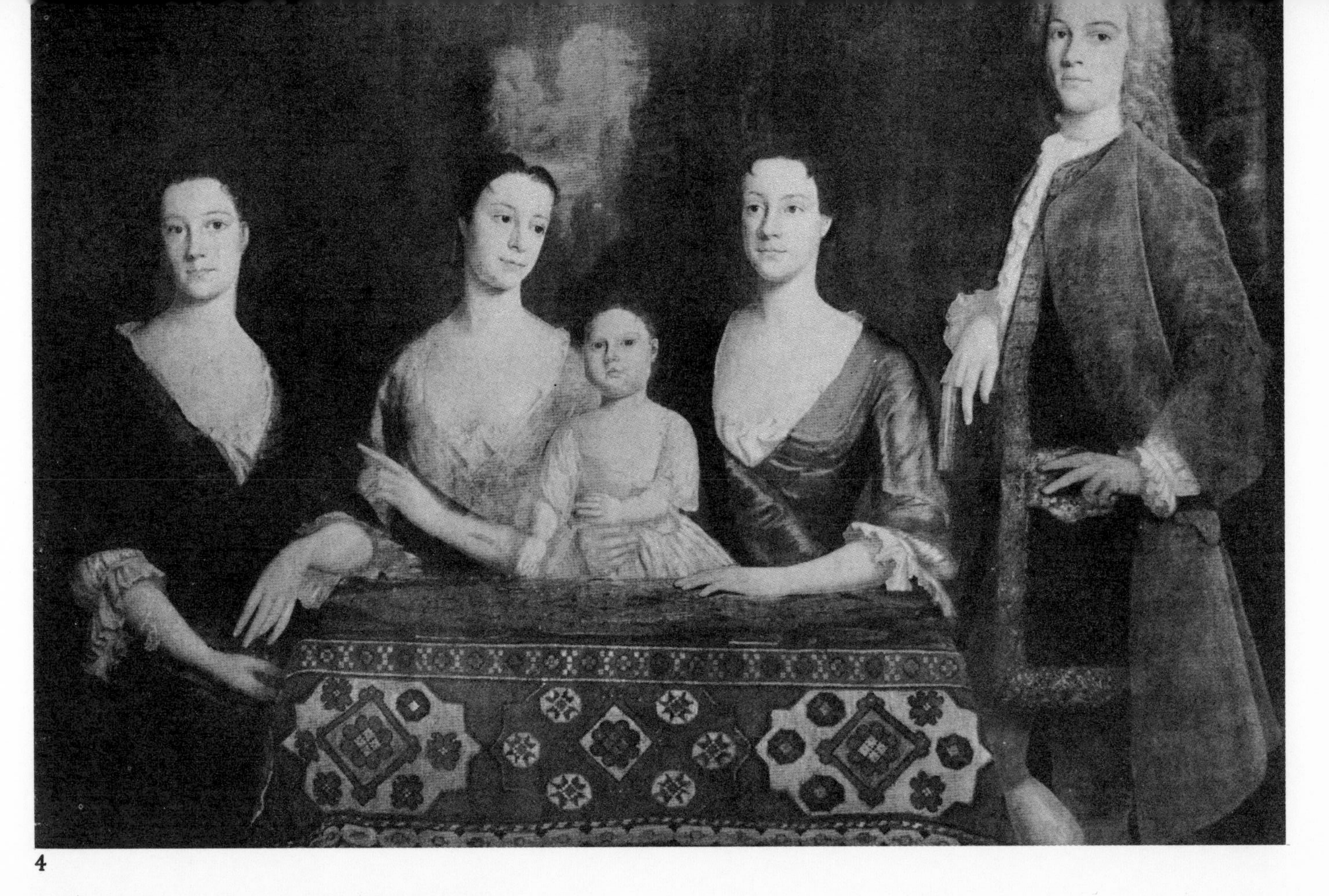

4

ROBERT FEKE: THE FAMILY OF ISAAC ROYALL

HN SINGLETON COPLEY: MRS. THOMAS BOYLSTON

6

JOHN SINGLETON COPLEY: THE DEATH OF THE EARL OF CHATHAM. ENGRAVING BY BARTOLOZZI

7

JOHN SINGLETON COPLEY: THE DEATH OF MAJOR PEIRSON

SINGLETON COPLEY: LORD HEATHFIELD

ketch for *The Defeat of the Floating Batteries at Gibraltar*

10

12

R. JOHN CLARK   10 PIETER NASON: A DOCTOR OF MEDECINE

NEW ENGLAND DIVINE, erroneously called *John Cotton*   12 JOHN DAVENPORT

14

16

HOLBEIN: LAIS CORINTHIACA 14 LADY MARGARET BEAUFORT

HOLBEIN: ANNE OF CLEVES 16 NICHOLAS HILLIARD: QUEEN ELIZABETH

17

18

19

20

17 VAN DYCK: KING CHARLES I 18 LELY: LADY BYRON

19 VAN SOMER: LADY APSLEY AND HER SON

20 VAN DYCK: THE WIFE AND DAUGHTER OF COLYNS DE NOLE

1 MARC GHAERAEDTS: LADY SIDNEY AND HER CHILDREN

2 PETER LELY: THE FAMILY OF SIR EDWARD HALES

BERT WALKER: OLIVER CROMWELL AND HIS SQUIRE

24

25

26

24 QUEEN ELIZABETH (The Cobham Portrait) 25 ELIZABETH PADDY WENSLEY 26 REBECCA RAWSON

27 28 29

27 UNKNOWN GERMAN LADY 28 MARGARET GIBBS 29 MRS. ELIZABETH DRAKE FULLER

30 GIRL WITH ROSES 31 HENRI ROUSSEAU: PAST AND PRESENT 32 HENRI ROUSSEAU: GIRL IN THE WOOD

34

33 LOUIS VIVIN: CONSEIL D'ETAT 34 JOHN KANE: ACROSS THE STRIP

36

35 JOSEPH PICKETT: CORYELL'S FERRY, 1776

36 ADOLF DIETRICH: A GARDEN (Detail)

37

38

37 LADY HOLDING A RED BOOK 38 GRANT WOOD: WOMAN WITH PLANTS

40

42

AS SMITH: 39 MAJOR THOMAS SAVAGE 40 CAPTAIN CURWEN
LFPORTRAIT 42 MARY CATHERINE SMITH

44

46

:REMIAH DUMMER: SELFPORTRAIT 44 KNELLER: THE EARL OF ROMNEY

REMIAH DUMMER: THE ARTIST'S WIFE 46 DAHL: MISS ELIZABETH EVELYN

48

50

PORTRAIT PANEL FROM A MUMMY OF THE FIRST CHRISTIAN CENTURY

REMBRANDT: SASKIA (?) 49 PORTRAIT PANEL FROM A MUMMY OF THE

IRD CHRISTIAN CENTURY 50 GERRET DUYCKINCK: THE ARTIST'S WIFE

51

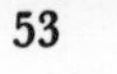

51 PIETER VANDERLYN: MRS. THOMAS VAN ALSTYNE 52 REVEREND THOMAS THACHER (?) 53 ANN POLLARD

54 55 56

54 JOHN SMIBERT: COPY AFTER VAN DYCK'S CARDINAL BENTIVOGLIO

55 JOHN SMIBERT: COSIMO III, GRAND DUKE OF TUSCANY (Probably after Magnasco)

56 MAGNASCO: DETAIL FROM "THE MUSIC LESSON" (Illustrating Magnasco's manner)

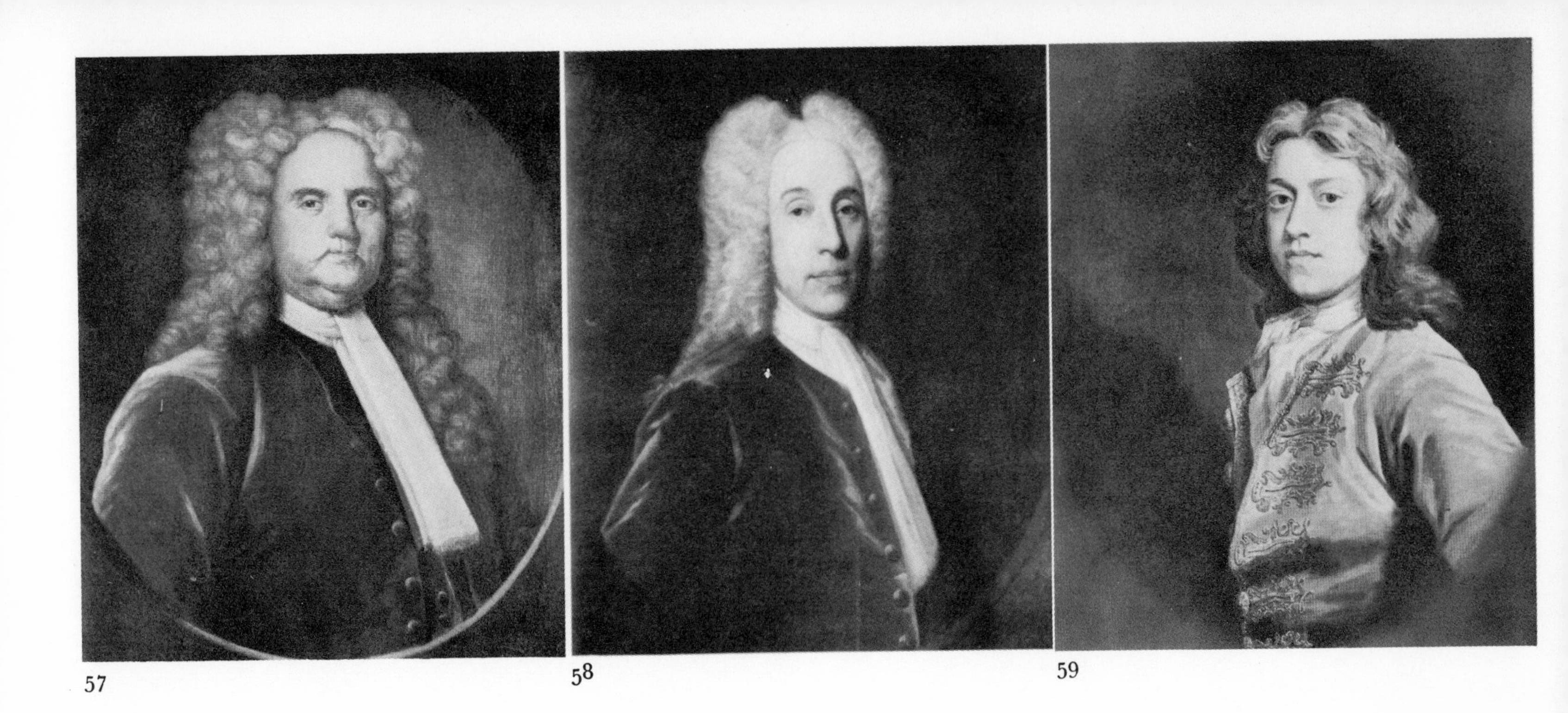

57 58 59

57 JOHN SMIBERT: NATHANIEL BYFIELD 58 JOHN SMIBERT: BENJAMIN PRATT 59 JAMES THORNHILL: SELFPORTRAIT

60

61

62

60 JOHN SMIBERT: WILLIAM BROWN 61 JOHN SMIBERT: MRS. WILLIAM BROWN 62 KNELLER: LADY MIDDLETON

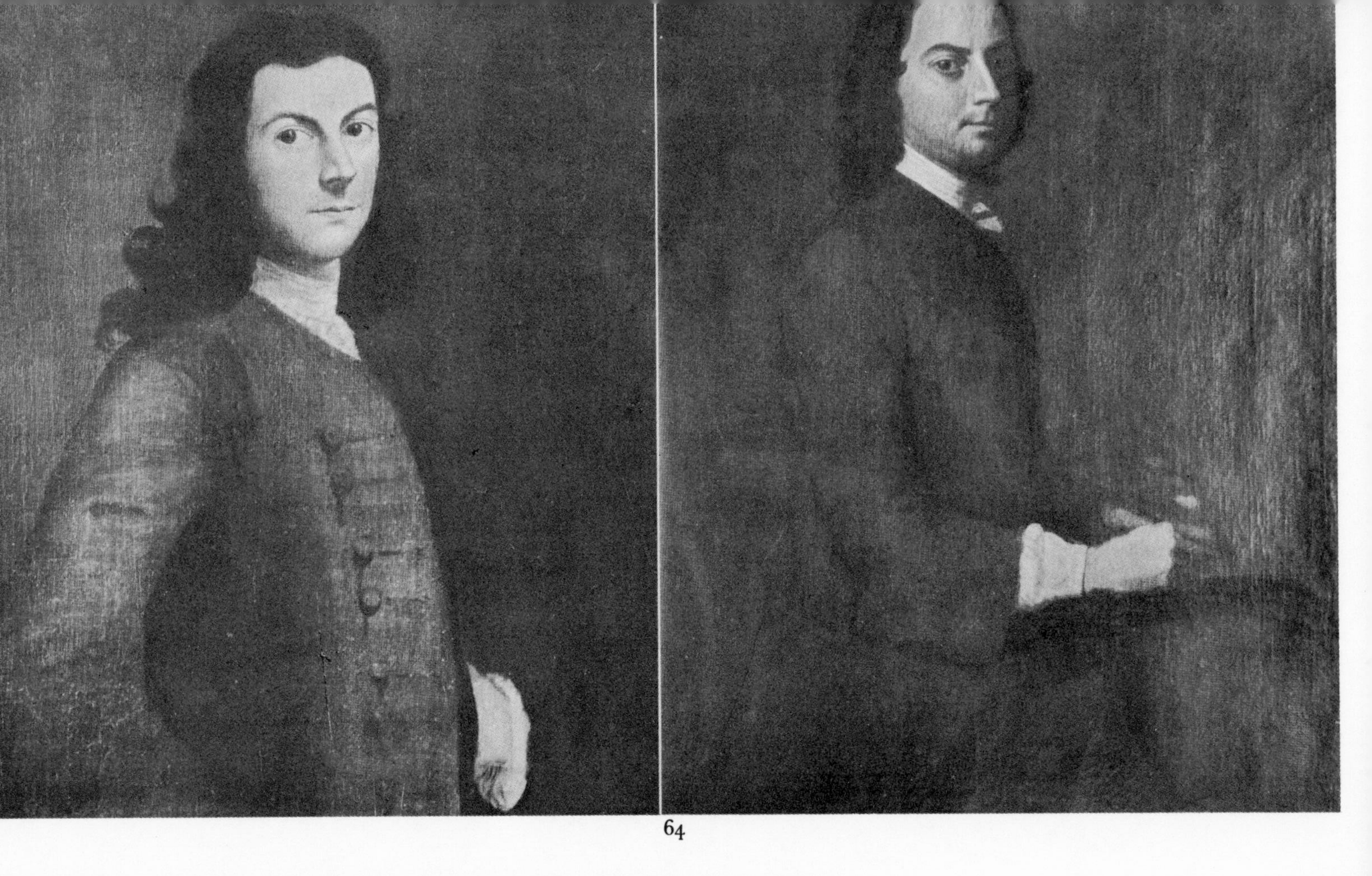

63 ROBERT FEKE: THE EARLY SELFPORTRAIT 64 ROBERT FEKE: THE LATE SELFPORTRAIT

65 ROBERT FEKE: MRS. TENCH FRANCIS  66 THOMAS HUDSON: MRS. HARVEY  67 JOSEPH BLACKBURN: MARGARET SYLVESTER CHESEBOROUGH

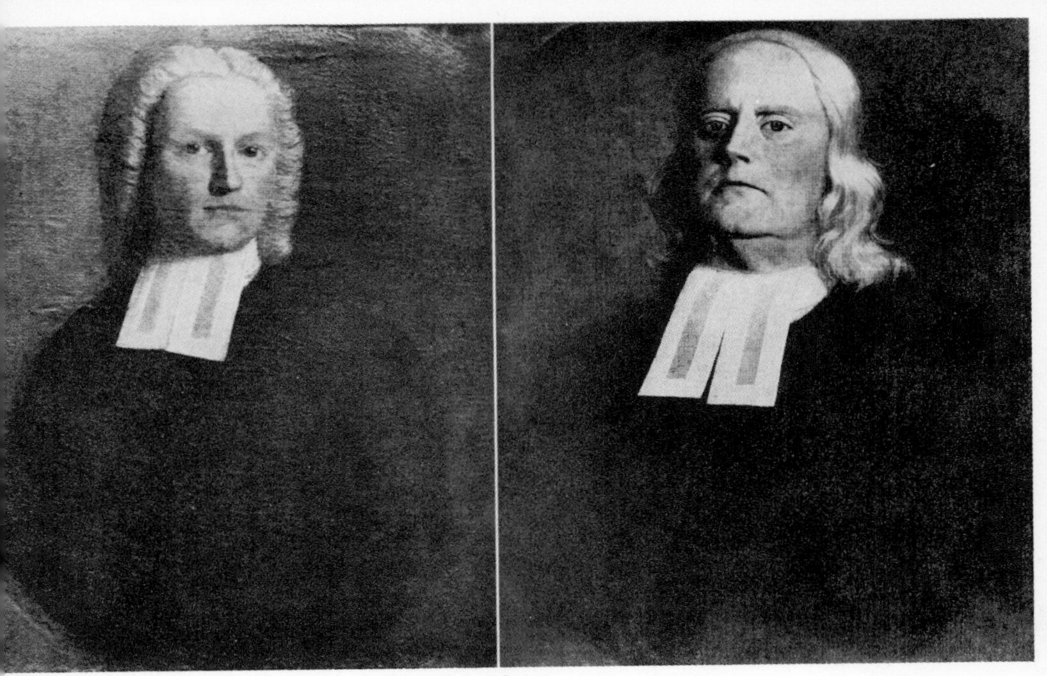

69

71

EKE: REV. JOHN CALLENDER 69 FEKE: REV. THOMAS HISCOX

EKE: JAMES BOWDOIN 71 HIGHMORE: GENTLEMAN IN A MURREY VELVET COAT

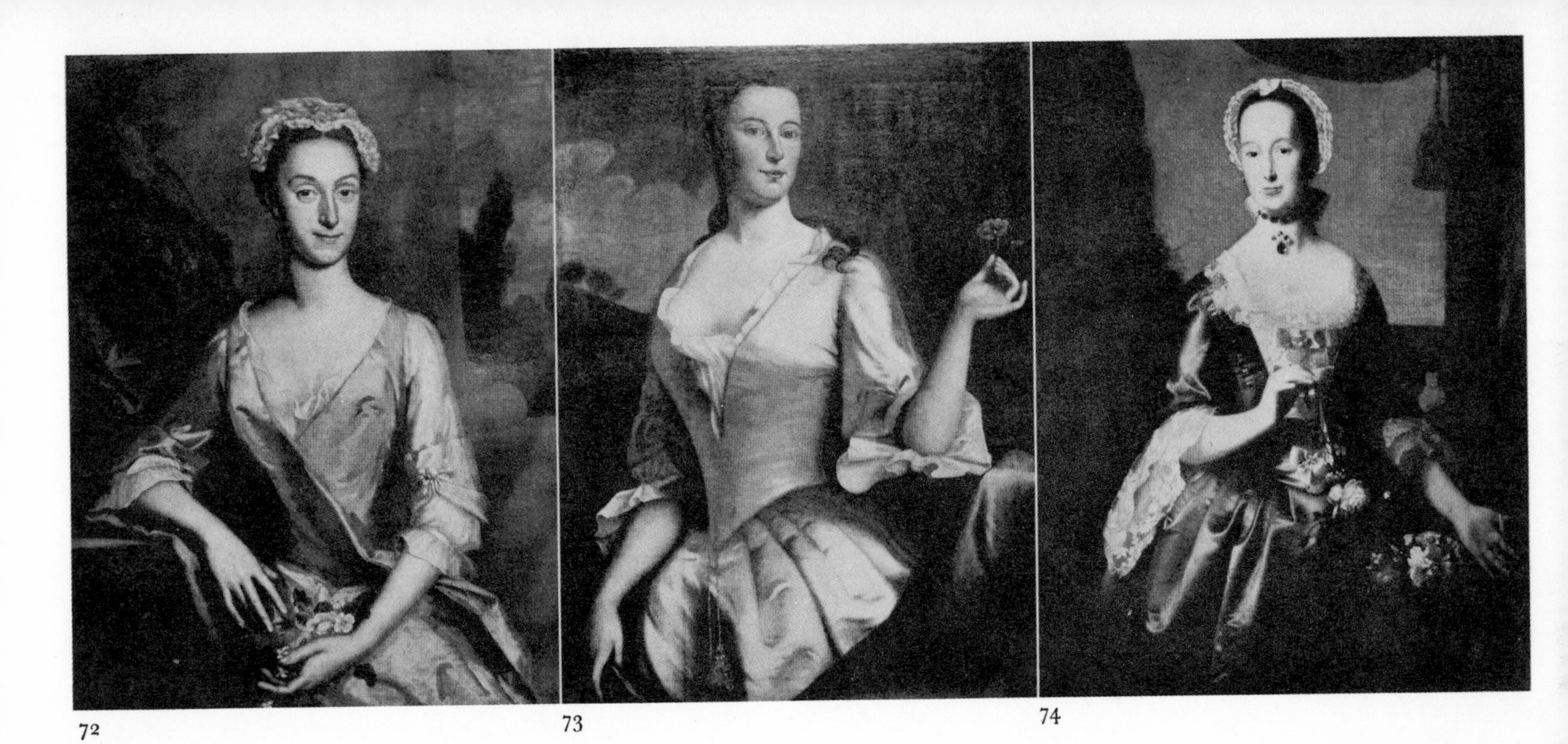

72 73 74

72 ROBERT FEKE: WILLIAMINA MOORE 73 ROBERT FEKE: MRS. JAMES TILGHMAN 74 JOHN S. COPLEY: MRS. METCALF BOWLER

75 JOHN SMIBERT: REVEREND JAMES MACSPARREN 76 COPLEY: REVEREND WILLIAM WELSTEED 77 COPLEY: EDWARD HOLYOKE

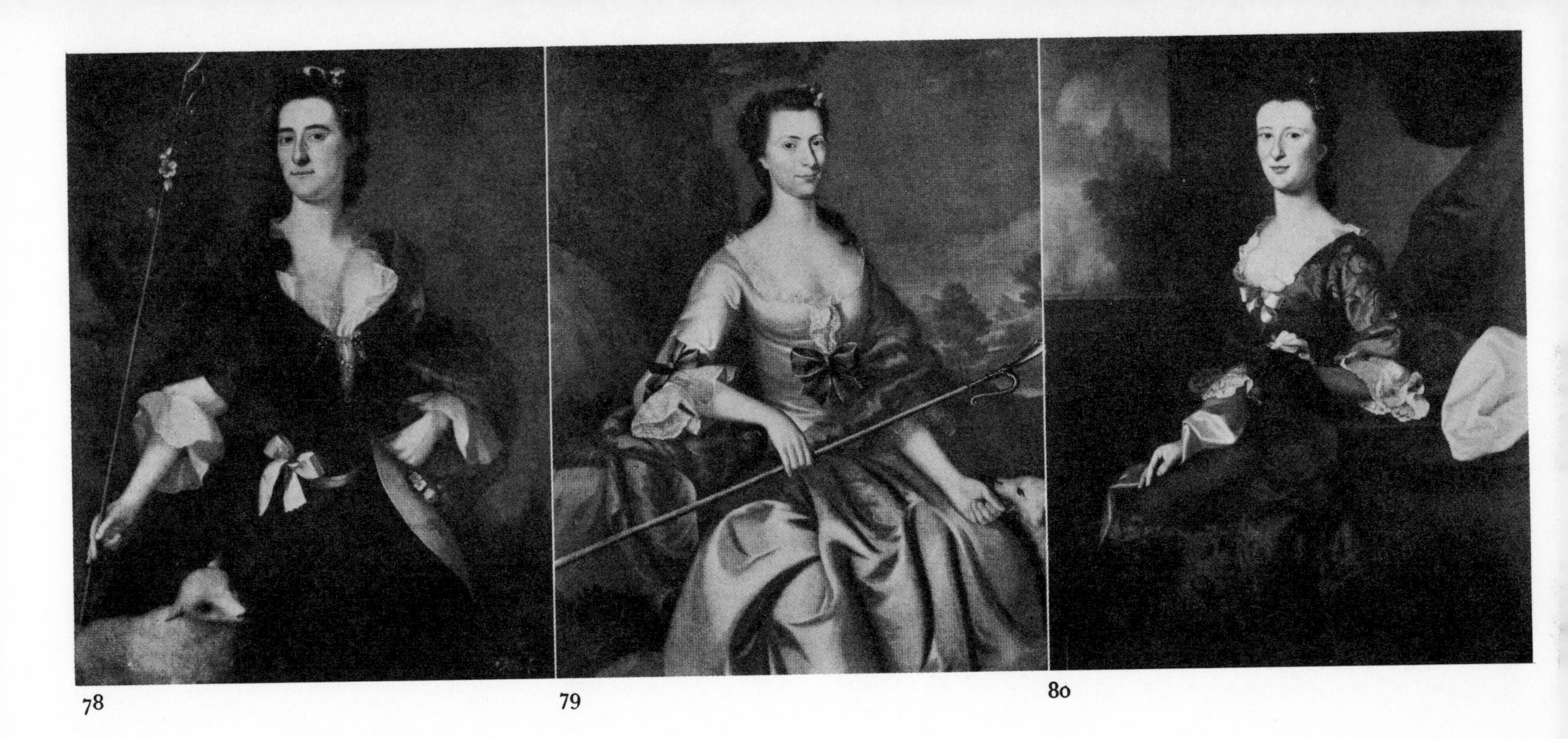

78 79 80

78 BLACKBURN: MARY SYLVESTER DERING 79 COPLEY: ANN TYNG SMELT 80 BLACKBURN: MRS. JONATHAN SIMPSON

82

84

BLACKBURN: JOSEPH DWIGHT 82 COPLEY: WILLIAM BRATTLE

VANDERBANCK: JOHN MICHAEL RYSBRACK 84 COPLEY: BENJAMIN PICKMAN

86

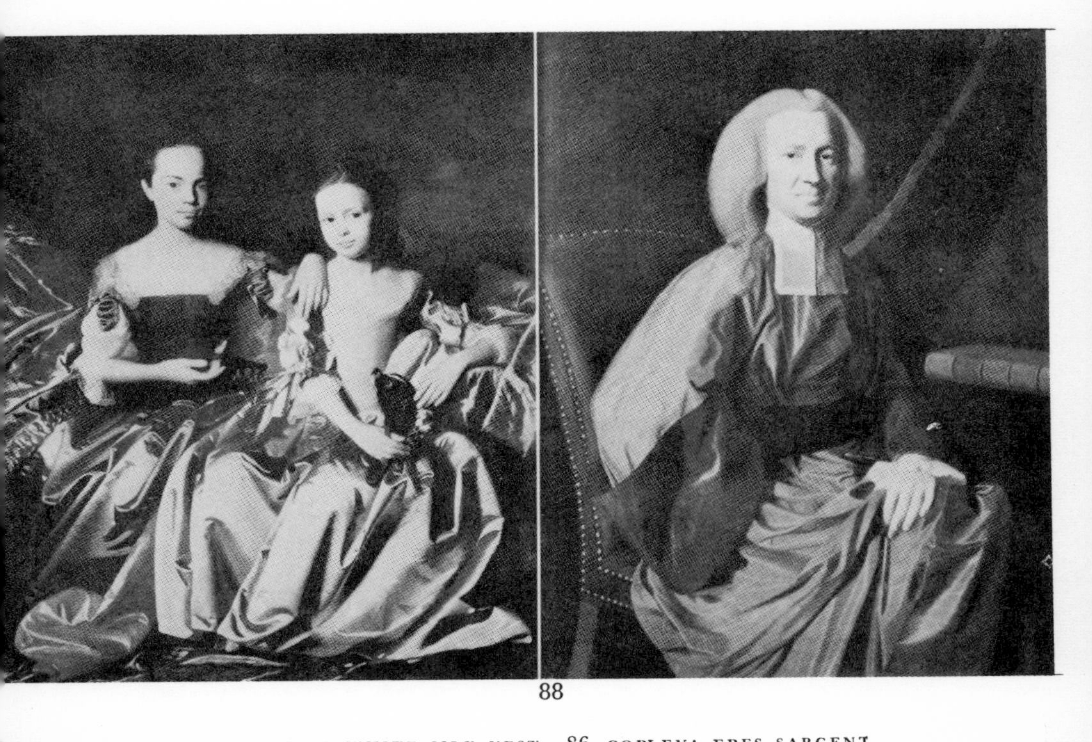

88

HIGHMORE: GENTLEMAN IN A WHITE SILK VEST 86 COPLEY: EPES SARGENT

COPLEY: MARY AND ELIZABETH ROYALL 88 COPLEY: JUDGE MARTIN HOWARD

89

90

JOHN SINGLETON COPLEY: 89 NATHANIEL HURD 90 THE BOY WITH THE SQUIRREL

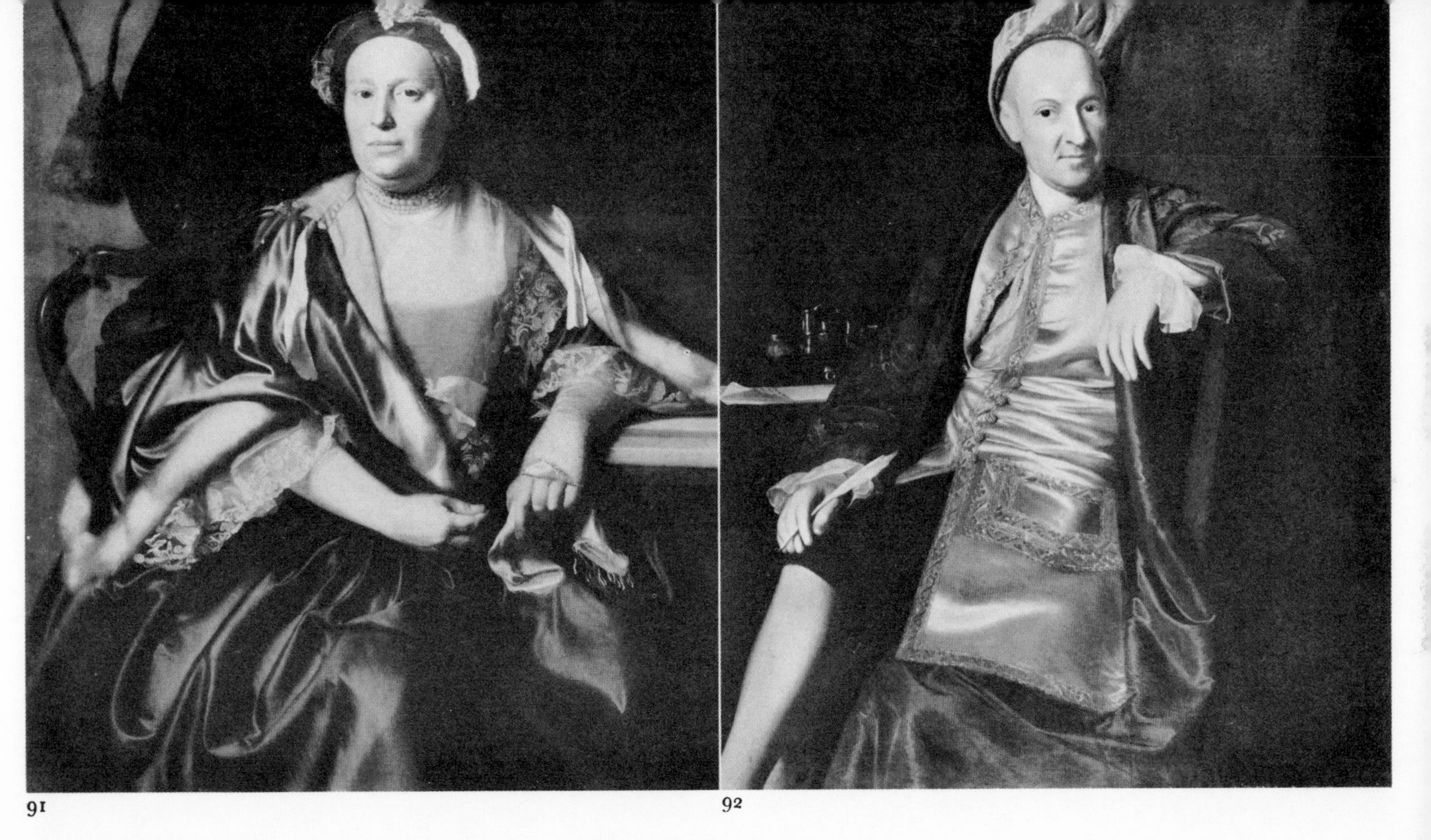

91

92

JOHN SINGLETON COPLEY: 91 MRS. ROBERT HOOPER 92 THOMAS BOYLSTON

NTON RAPHAEL MENGS: MOUNT PARNASSUS

ENJAMIN WEST: THE DEATH OF WOLFE

96

RAPHAEL: GROUP FROM "THE SCHOOL OF ATHENS"

RAPHAEL: THE HOLY FAMILY (MADONNA CANIGIANI)

98

JAMIN WEST: 97 LADY BEAUCHAMPS PROCTOR 98 ALDERMAN SAWBRIDGE
THE DRUMMOND FAMILY

BENJAMIN WEST: ERASISTRATUS DISCOVERS THE LOVE OF ANTIOCHUS

R STRATONICE 101 JACQUES LOUIS DAVID: STRATONICE

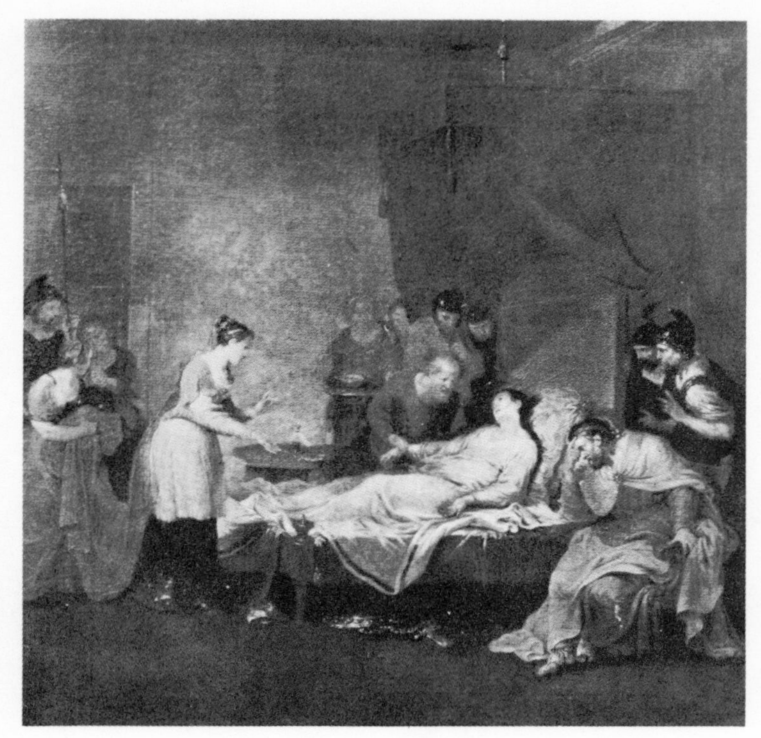

102

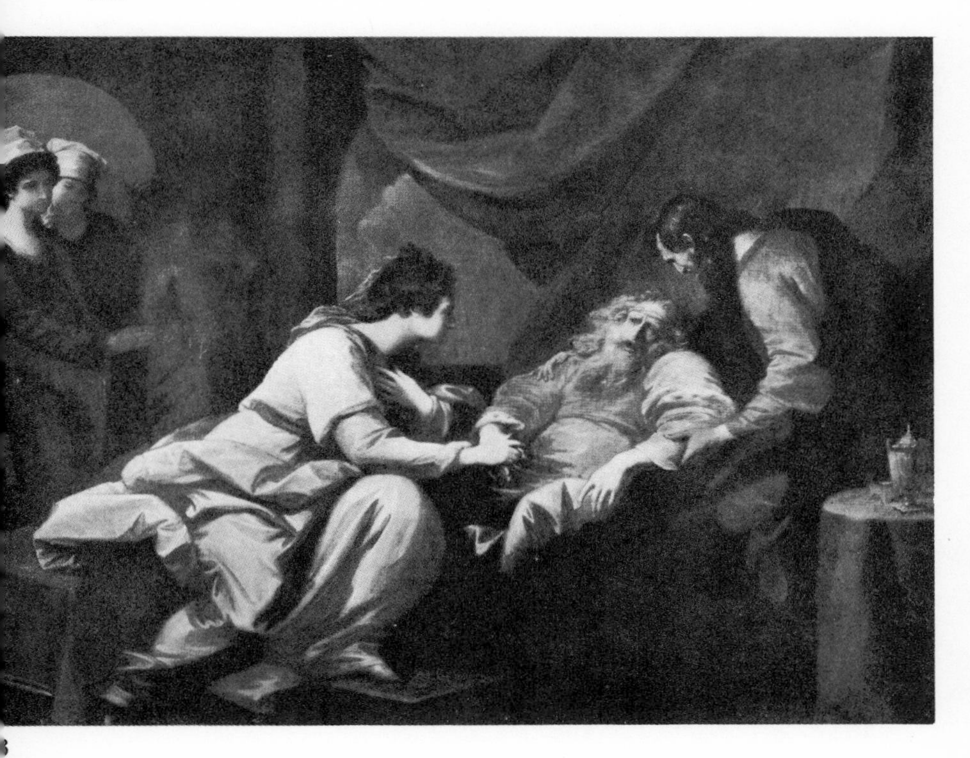

JANUARIUS ZICK: STRATONICE

BENJAMIN WEST: CORDELIA MAKES HERSELF KNOWN TO KING LEAR

104

105

106

104 GRAVELOT: ILLUSTRATION OF A PLAY BY CORNEILLE  105 COPLEY: VENUS, MARS, AND VULCAN

106 MARTINI: ILLUSTRATION OF AN OPERATIC LIBRETTO

107

108

109

JOHN S. COPLEY: 107 COL. JEREMIAH LEE

108 BRASS CROSBY, LORD MAYOR OF LONDON 109 MR. AND MRS. RALPH IZARD

IO

IO JOHN SINGLETON COPLEY: THE ROYAL PRINCESSES

111

112

111 COPLEY: COMPOSITIONAL DRAWING FOR THE DEATH OF THE EARL OF CHATHAM

112 COPLEY: STUDY FOR THE MAIN GROUP OF THE DEATH OF THE EARL OF CHATHAM

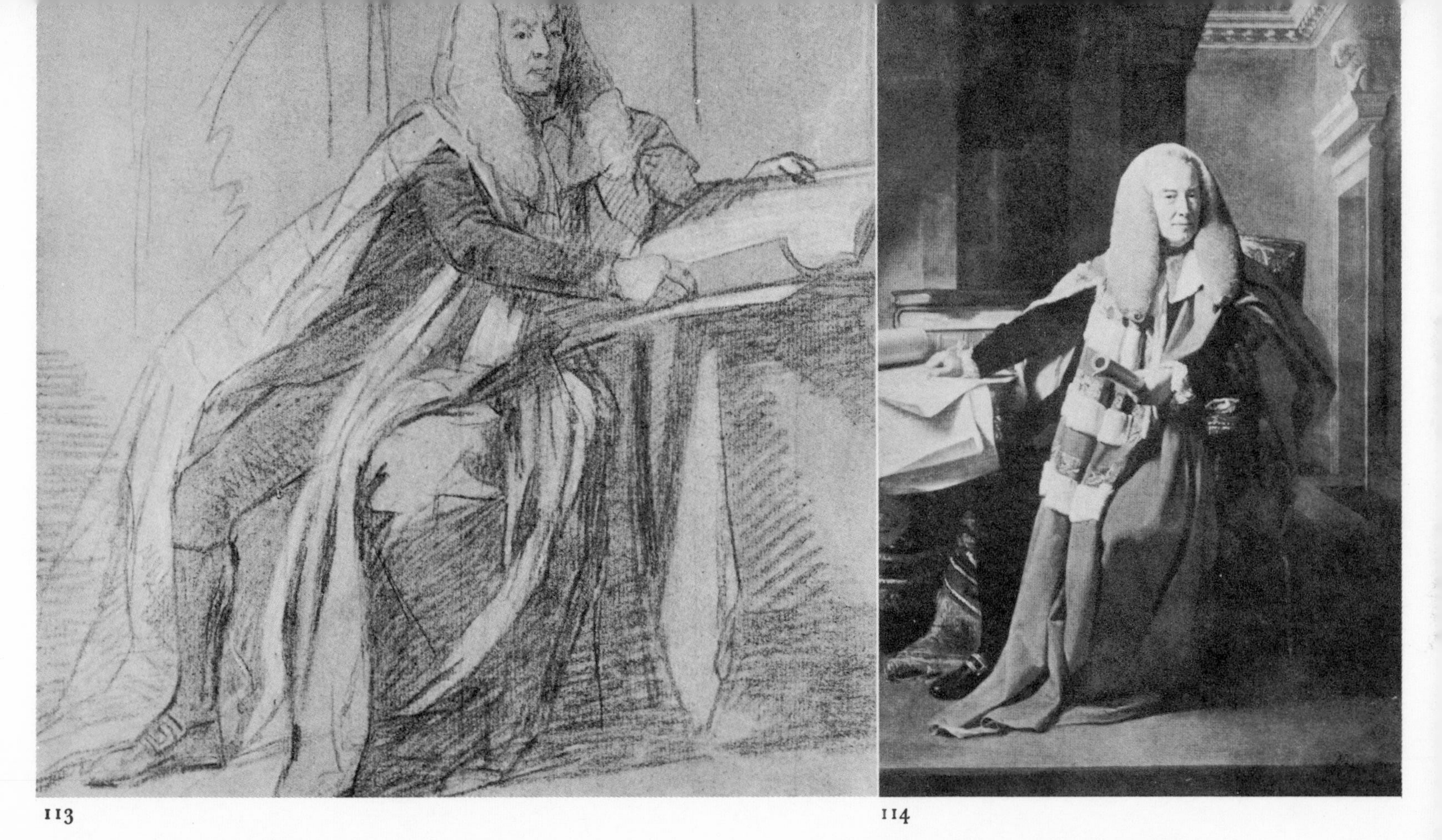

113

114

COPLEY: 113 LORD MANSFIELD, DRAWING FOR THE DEATH OF THE EARL OF CHATHAM 114 PORTRAIT OF LORD MANSFIELD

5

6

5 COPLEY: THE DEFEAT OF THE FLOATING BATTERIES AT GIBRALTAR (MONOCHROME)
6 COPLEY: COMPOSITIONAL DRAWING FOR THE DEFEAT OF GIBRALTAR

:OPLEY: CHARLES I DEMANDS THE IMPEACHED MEMBERS OF PARLIAMENT

OHN TRUMBULL: THE FAMILY OF JONATHAN TRUMBULL

:ALPH EARL: MRS. BENJAMIN TALLMADGE WITH HER CHILDREN

# Index

# INDEX

# INDEX

# INDEX

# INDEX

# INDEX

# INDEX

# INDEX

# INDEX